enigma
books

General
Paul Aussaresses

The Battle
of the Casbah

Terrorism
and Counter-Terrorism in Algeria
1955-1957

enigma books

enigma books
580 Eighth Avenue, New York, NY 10018
www.enigmabooks.com

Originally published in French under the title:
SERVICES SPÉCIAUX Algérie 1955-1957

Translated by Robert L. Miller

© enigma books 2002
© Perrin 2001
First English language edition
ISBN 1-929631-12-X
Printed in The United States of America

Library of Congress Cataloging in Publication Data

Aussaresses, Paul.
   [Services spéciaux.]
   The battle of the Casbah : terrorism and counter-terrorism in
Algeria 1955-1957 / Paul Aussaresses ; translated by Robert L.
Miller.— 1st English language ed.

   Includes index.

   ISBN: 1-929631-12-X

1. Algeria—History—Revolution, 1954-1962—Personal narratives,
French. 2. Algeria—History—Revolution, 1954-1962—Atrocities. 3.
Aussaresses, Paul. 4. France. Service de documentation extérieur et de
contre-espionnage. Service Action—History—20th century. I. Miller,
Robert L. (Robert Lawrence), 1945- II. Title. III. Title: Services
spéciaux.

DT295.3.A8 A87 2002   965/.0468

The Battle of the Casbah

Table of Contents

Publisher's Introduction

Is it ever justifiable to torture a suspected terrorist if that is the *only* way to save hundreds or even thousands of innocent people whose lives are in imminent danger?

On January 23, 2002 on CBS' *60 Minutes*, Mike Wallace asked French General Paul Aussaresses whether he would use torture today to force Al Qaeda suspects, and specifically Zacarias Moussaoui (the suspected twentieth man in Mohamed Atta's airplane hijacking team, scheduled to go on trial in a Virginia Federal Court), to reveal what he knows about other terrorists and their future plans. The General, responding in English, said without hesitation: "It seems to me that it's obvious." His message in this book is clear: no struggle against terrorism can succeed without the willingness on the part of the potential target to use every available weapon, including torture, to fight the enemy. On the same *60 Minutes* segment Harvard law professor Alan Dershowitz agreed that the use of torture is justified in certain drastic circumstances, namely the "ticking bomb scenario," concluding that, following the terror attacks on the United States, "experiences change our conception of rights." Other critics on the same program strongly disagreed with Aussaresses and Dershowitz on moral and legal grounds.

The following pages will come as a shock to the reader. They deal with events that happened almost half a century ago in Algeria, a land few Americans are acquainted with. But after September 11, 2001 those terrible events and the questions they raise suddenly appear frighteningly relevant.

In the spring of 2001 French public opinion was jolted upon reading the facts as revealed for the first time by Paul Aussaresses, a retired General of 83, who had served in the French army in Algeria from 1954 to 1957. Many allegations of torture during the Algerian war had been leveled at French army units by some of their victims in the past but none of the alleged perpetrators of torture had ever come forward to describe in detail the circumstances and the reasons behind what now appears to have been government policy.

The Algerian war ended in 1962 with a political solution worked out by the government of General Charles de Gaulle and the FLN (National Liberation Front), resulting in the independence of Algeria. France thereby lost a vast territory in North Africa, while about one million French residents were forced to abandon most of their possessions, leaving in panic during the summer of that year. The war resulted in over 30,000 French dead and probably as many as half a million Algerians.

General Paul Aussaresses recounts how, under instructions from the French government from 1955 to 1957, he became a key covert figure in the counter-terrorist struggle. Through a combination of intelligence work, the use of torture, and summary executions, Aussaresses describes how he broke the FLN insurgency in the city of Algiers and rid the Casbah of innumerable terror cells. It is significant to note that the identity of Paul Aussaresses was unknown to all but a handful of people. His name does not even appear in most books dealing with the Algerian war and the role he played is described here for the first time, making this book an invaluable historical document.

Terrorism clearly fits into the category of a particularly cruel form of psychological warfare primarily targeting civilians. The Algerian war that France waged from 1954 to 1962 against the FLN did not just suddenly happen, nor was it an isolated event. The entire colonial system (French, British, Belgian, Dutch, and Portuguese) had come under severe pressure since the Second World War. The defining moment for France was its defeat by Nazi Germany in 1940, and the humiliating armistice with Hitler. The importance of that event was not lost on the young nationalists aspiring to independence, from Morocco to Indochina. By the end of the Second World War events had taken a violent turn in Indochina, where the conflict lasted from 1946 until the defeat of the French garrison at Dien Bien Phu in May 1954, effectively ending French presence in Southeast Asia.

In Algeria, which was considered an integral part of metropolitan France and not a colony or a protectorate, a bloody revolt broke out in the rural town of Sétif on May 8, 1945 (the very day World War Two ended). The French army and local police forces crushed the rebellion, at the price of a violent repression that left deep scars within the Algerian Muslim population. The events of Sétif were a warning shot to the nationalists and the French alike.

Other warnings went unheeded by French authorities, including the relatively moderate calls by nationalists, such as Ferhat Abbas, for a more liberal policy toward the vast majority of Algerian Muslims, who were not granted either the benefit of French nationality or equal voting rights. Ferhat Abbas eventually became President of the Algerian government-in-exile, which was part of the FLN, in Tunis.

Other momentous changes within the Arab world created growing ferment, encouraging the Algerians to forge ahead with their plans to seek independence. In Egypt in 1952 young nationalist Egyptian army officers overthrew King Farouk and the monarchy. Colonel Gamal Abdel Nasser quickly took over the military junta and actively encouraged Arab nationalism outside Egypt. Closer to Algeria, in neighboring Morocco on August 20, 1953, Sultan Sidi Mohammed Ben Youssef was deposed by French administrators allied with traditionalist tribes from the south. The Sultan, who favored the more mild nationalist elements, was sent off with his family into exile to the remote island of Madagascar. Soon Morocco experienced a steady wave of urban terrorism and guerrilla attacks aimed at French settlers. The same violent unrest was spreading to Tunisia, the oldest French protectorate in North Africa. By the end of 1955 the French governments of Edgar Faure, and then Guy Mollet, were ready to grant broad autonomy evolving rapidly into full independence to Morocco and Tunisia in March 1956, while vowing to hold firm on Algeria.

On November 1, 1954 a series of violent attacks erupted, mostly in eastern Algeria, exclusively targeting French citizens. On August 20, 1955, following nearly one year of increasing violence, a series of extremely brutal attacks again rocked Morocco and Algeria with hundreds of casualties.

In his memoir General Aussaresses describes probably the most horrific of the bloody incidents that took place that day in the port town of Philippeville, where he was stationed as an intelligence officer. Hundreds of armed rebels attempted to seize the city center, seeking to kill as many French citizens as possible, and were thwarted only because of advance intelligence Aussaresses had gathered, using methods that often involved torture.

By the end of 1956 the situation had worsened throughout Algeria, especially within the main urban center of Algiers, which was experiencing almost daily terrorist attacks. Aussaresses was given the mission by General Jacques Massu to crush the terror network using all available means. It is absolutely clear from this book and in conversations between the author and this publisher that the highest officials of the French government in Paris at the time had decided upon the policy of all-out counter-terrorism that General Massu and then Major Aussaresses were implementing. From January 1957 until the summer of that year, Aussaresses dutifully carried out his mission. Existing books dealing with the French government's role during the Algerian war seek to portray certain army officers as acting on their own initiative or even against the spirit of governmental policy. This memoir squarely contradicts those statements: according to Aussaresses officials at the highest level were ordering and supporting the actions of the French army. The descriptions he offers of the famous "battle of Algiers" make up the main segment of this book. The core of the battle, the key to control of the city, was the Casbah, and in the end it was inside the Casbah that the main leaders of the terrorist cells of the FLN were located and either arrested or killed.

Torture or, more often, the mere threat of torture, would usually lead to a confession and to vital information that in turn could prevent more bloodshed and more civilian deaths. Because of this book a controversy has erupted involving Yacef Saadi, a top FLN leader who was arrested in the Casbah. Mr. Saadi, now a senator in Algeria and considered a hero of the revolution, is accused by General Aussaresses of having volunteered to French paratroopers, without ever being tortured, the exact location in the Casbah where the legendary terrorist Ali-la-Pointe was hiding. This revelation has caused some embarrassment to the Algerian government and to Yacef Saadi, who denies the allegation. The death of Ali-la-Pointe effectively ended the battle of Algiers in a victory for the French army.

By mid-1957 General Aussaresses had completed his mission in Algeria and moved on to other assignments. He never discussed his part in the war until the publication of this book in France in May 2001, which caused an immediate furor and led to a civil lawsuit against him, his publisher, and his editor by several human rights organizations. French politicians immediately reacted to the outcry: President Jacques Chirac ordered the General stripped of the Legion of Honor and forbidden to wear his uniform. Even though General Aussaresses, along with everyone associated with the war in Algeria, was granted a general amnesty, the complaint filed against his book states that Paul Aussaresses is guilty of "justifying war crimes." The prosecutor said that "this book justifies in a shocking and totally unjustifiable way the excesses that were perpetrated during the Algerian war." On January 25, 2002 the court sentenced General Aussaresses, his French publisher, and his editor to pay a fine. All three have filed an appeal.

The basis of the complaint, that the General was unrepentant and "justifies war crimes," would never stand up in an American or British court because it is tantamount to censorship and, in America at least, a denial of the First Amendment rights of free speech. In an editorial published in the French news magazine *Le Point* on December 14, 2001, liberal French writer and social critic Bernard-Henry Lévy took a strong position against the implied censorship in this case, especially where freedom of expression is concerned:

> It inhibits any publisher who should hypothetically discover tomorrow the confessions of an Auschwitz guard, of a KGB agent or a former Khmer Rouge leader, the memoirs of someone like Maurice Papon, or any repentant kamikaze, from publishing them without fear of being indicted as an accomplice to the crime. It gives the judge power over the historian... it reintroduces something that looks strangely like a form of censorship... The war in Algeria is today, at least as much as Vichy, the black hole of French memory.

In America, in Israel, in Northern Ireland, as well as the rest of Europe, Russia, India, Pakistan, the Philippines, and a host of other countries, the new terrorism has become brutally real and the new war on terrorism has many of its roots in places like Algeria. It must be remembered that since the 1990s Algeria has again been torn by a long and bloody civil war of terror, this time between Islamic extremists and the Algerian FLN regime. In cases such as Algeria or the Middle East, terror is almost always a tool cynically used to convince a wavering population to join the boldest and most aggressive side, the one held up as most likely to win. Nationalist independence movements after the Second World War have operated in many instances on two levels. The

official political movement, which is openly seeking a negotiated solution with the colonial or occupying power, and
the clandestine terrorist organization that keeps up the pressure on the ground, even when negotiations are in progress—
a procedure used time and again by the FLN in Algeria, the
Viet Minh in Indochina, North Korea, North Vietnam, and
in the Middle East to this day, with tragic consequences.

Nations react to danger in their own ways, with a mix of
the instinct for self-preservation and the legal justification
of self-defense.

As Walter Laqueur writes in his book *The New Terrorism*
(1999):

> When terrorism becomes a real danger those engaging
> in it will no longer be able to run and hide, but will be treated
> by those attacked as they see fit, as a *hostis*, an enemy of hu-
> mankind and thus outside the law.

This memoir is an important historical document written by a key participant in a type of war America has never
experienced until now. The questions it raises are difficult
and complex, and often deal with very hard political and
moral choices. We trust the reader to reach his or her own
uncensored conclusion.

Robert L. Miller
Publisher

French Publisher's Note

General Paul Aussaresses first mentioned his memoirs of the Algerian war in early 2001 in the course of an interview published in the Paris daily, *Le Monde*. We decided that it was important to publish the story of this shadowy but central participant in that conflict.

Since that initial interview, there have been many reactions, some of them sounding like a nostalgic defense of the past, others by persons who felt the need to justify their role, as well as those critics who harshly condemned the author of this book. The first-hand memoir offered here has never been published before. Forty years after those events this book contributes to our understanding of the terribly complex reality of a time that is still very close to us today.

Author's Foreword

Like many other fellow soldiers who had fought in Algeria I had decided to remain silent but not to forget. My past service as an intelligence officer in the Special Services of the French Republic made that an obvious choice. Furthermore, since my mission in Algeria had remained secret, I could have hidden behind that protective veil. Therefore, it will come as quite a surprise that 40 years later I have decided to place my experience of the very serious events on record dealing with the methods used to fight terrorism, and in particular the use of torture and summary executions.

I know that the story that follows will shock some readers—those who were in the know and would have preferred that I remain silent, just as those who didn't know and would have preferred never to find out. I think it is useful that the facts should now be told and since, as the reader will discover, I was involved in some of the most crucial events of the Algerian war, I now feel that it is my duty to tell the whole story. The page must be written and read before we can turn it over forever.

What I did in Algeria was undertaken for my country in good faith, even though I didn't enjoy it. One must never regret anything accomplished in the line of a duty one believes in. Only too often today condemning others means acquiring a certificate of morality for just about anyone. I write only about myself in my memoir. I don't attempt to justify my actions, but only to explain that once a country demands that its army fight an enemy who is using terror to compel an indifferent population to join its ranks and provoke a repression that will in turn outrage international public opinion, it becomes impossible for that army to avoid using extreme measures.

I pass no judgment on others and certainly not on my former enemies. I often wonder what would happen today in a French town if there were daily attacks taking innocent lives. Would we not be hearing after a few weeks the top leaders of the country demanding that the attacks be stopped by any and all means required?

May the readers of this book remember that it is easier to judge in haste than to understand, and simpler to ask for forgiveness than to state the facts.

1

Soual's Way

On November 1, 1954, All Saints Day, I was still on duty in Paris at the Action Service (*Action Service*) of the SDECE. On the same day, I was ordered to transfer to the 41st airborne brigade stationed at Philippeville in Algeria. That very day a few hundred Algerians came down from the Aurès Mountains and organized scores of spectacular attacks to start the revolt of what it has been fashionable to refer to since then as the "Muslim people." But the majority of the population, which was made up for the most part of ordinary people trying to make a living, did not recognize itself in these small bands that were often feuding among themselves, a strange mix of intellectuals and small-time crooks.

The government of Pierre Mendès-France, which had been formed in June, following the defeat at Dien Bien Phu, had been until then rather tolerant toward the autonomist political movements in French North Africa. These events determined a change in attitude and the government decided to be firm, seeking to reassure the French settlers in Algeria. Pierre Mendès-France, therefore, in addressing Parliament on November 12 stated that the government would never agree to any kind of compromise. François Mitterrand, who was minister of the interior and responsible for the French administrative departments in Algeria, felt that local police forces were unable to maintain "French republican" order. He dispatched his chief of staff to the ministry of defense, requesting regular army troops and also stated very clearly on the same day, November 12, to the members of Parliament: "I will not agree to negotiate with the enemies of the homeland. The only negotiation is war!"

That was how the conflict became official, even though it was never referred to as anything more than a peacekeeping operation. Reinforcements, including conscripts, were sent to Algeria. But secretly within the circles of the shadowy men of intelligence we knew that this war had started a long time before. The government issuing our orders also knew it full well. I served for one year in the *Action Service* of the SDECE, where I had temporary command during the spring of 1954, while my boss, Jacques Morlanne, was away on a mission. The SDECE was beginning to prepare covert initiatives to prevent the rebels from being supplied with weapons. Had I remained at the "dairy" (the nickname we used for the SDECE), I would have no doubt taken part in one of those missions. However, circumstances took me to the spot where I was to participate directly in military operations.

Morlanne told me this was just a brief tour of duty in a regular army unit that would help my career along and speed up my promotion. My boss was prone to being quite a wishful thinker. He had a soft spot for me and yet one day I was so incensed against him that I really almost choked him in his office. He begged me to think of my wife and kids so that I'd let go of him. But Morlanne was not someone to bear grudges and since that incident he had named me his successor.

Even though I had been appointed, as of November 1, 1954, to the 41st brigade, I had to wait until the end of January 1955 to board a ship in Marseille bound for Philippeville. I felt quite calm as I hurried up the gangplank paying no attention to the dark clouds covering the sky, announcing a rough crossing. I might say that I even felt euphoric. In spite of my uniform I was humming the song *Le Déserteur* by Boris Vian with relish because the radio had banned playing it. I was 36 and even though I don't like the title that much, I was what they call a "secret agent." Naturally whenever I was asked what I did for a living my answer was captain in the French army and, if they wanted to know more, that I was in the airborne infantry. Beyond that I was married with children and led a quiet and normal private life.

Nothing in my background could have even hinted at the kind of adventures I was experiencing. Certainly not the first prize in Latin translation I won at the general regents exams, nor my years in the preparatory classes at the Lycée Montaigne in Bordeaux, where my classmates included Robert Escarpit, who later became a pacifist university professor and an editorial writer at *Le Monde*; and André Mandouze, who went on to become one of the leaders of those intellectuals who were critical of the French army and favorable to the "just cause" of the FLN. My degree was in Latin, Greek, and philology and all those studies would have been more conducive to a quiet career as a university professor or, if that didn't work out, as a diplomat.

That would have been more to my father's liking. He was an historian, and a friend of the novelist Colette. Somehow he wound up becoming a prefect in the local government administration, holding various cabinet positions until finally turning into an administrator at a major provincial daily newspaper. The times when I used to recite to my father from memory Cicero's *Pro Archia* or Lenau's *Don Juan* seemed so far away. The war broke out in 1939 and on November 27, 1942 I made one of the most important decisions of my life when, after making the army my career and deciding to join Charles de Gaulle, I volunteered for the special services. I was therefore going to embark, for my country and undercover, on a career demanding the kind of behavior that is banned by any ordinary moral code, and is often considered illegal and classified as an official secret. It meant stealing, killing, destroying, and terrorizing others. I was taught how to pick locks, how to murder without leaving a trace, to lie, to be indifferent to any pain inflicted upon me as well as to the pain of other people, to forget everything and make sure everyone forgot me as well. All this was done in the name of France.

Officially the assignment to Algeria had nothing to do with a new mission. However, once you have been inside such an environment you can never completely shake off its influence. Once you have been a member of the special services everything you do later on will always appear to have a whiff of mystery. I had held a strategic position at the SDECE and for a few weeks I had even been temporarily in command of 29 (the code name for the *Action Service*). We had been going through a rough year at the end of the war in Indochina, and the fear of a looming Soviet invasion had led to the creation of weapons caches to organize the resistance should the enemy occupy the country. The armed struggle in Algeria had come on top of all these concerns, but at the time, according to the formula the authorities were endlessly repeating, Algeria was part of France and the SDECE wasn't chartered, at least theoretically, to take action inside French territory.

At first we began taking action outside the borders of France and those operations increased once I left. The objective was to neutralize those who sold weapons to the FLN and stop the ships used to transport them. Thanks to the operations of René Taro and his team (Taro was a naval officer within the *Action Service* specializing in sabotage), many ships had sunk without apparent reason in the North Sea and the Mediterranean. Other teams had dealt with the arms merchants, many of whom had suddenly developed strange illnesses or had become unexpectedly suicidal. We still had to act directly against the rebels themselves and for that we needed a presence in Algeria. I didn't know whether this assignment to Philippeville was a new mission, a low blow cooked up for me by Morlanne, or simply a short interruption in my career as a spook. If it was a mission, I had no idea what it consisted of.

I had been deeply involved with the special services for over ten years. In January 1943, de Gaulle had sent me to liberate General Cochet, a World War I air ace who had been interned by Vichy at a prison camp near Vals-les-Bains for having insulted Marshal Pétain and his entourage in an article published in an underground newspaper. That mission was to land me in a Spanish jail in Pamplona for eight months. As part of the Jedburgh I was involved in other missions out of London. I parachuted over the Ariège region in a British captain's uniform to give assistance to the partisan fighters of the Iberian anarchist federation. In April 1945 I parachuted behind the lines once again but this time in a German uniform just outside Berlin. After barely avoiding the *Scharnhorst* division, an elite navy unit, I was arrested by the Soviet troops of Marshal Zhukov, who mistook me for a French volunteer in the *Charlemagne* SS division. At the last minute I was barely able to avoid being shot in the back of the head by the NKVD. After that I worked for Jacques Foccart before going to Indochina. I returned and founded the 11th Shock at Fort Montlouis, near Perpignan.* Back in Indochina I carried out missions behind Viet Minh lines and even infiltrated secretly into China to negotiate with the Chinese Nationalists. I had more recently taken charge of the instruc-

---

* After setting up the Action Service of the SDECE, I was also to be the founder of the 11th Shock paratrooper battalion on September 1, 1946 and remained in charge until 1948. The 11th Shock battalion was the commando unit of the Action Service; it was renamed 11th Demi-Brigade of shock paratroopers in October 1955, and finally broken up on December 31, 1963. Following the Rainbow Warrior incident, the unit was revived by François Mitterrand on November 1, 1985, only to be terminated once again in 1995 and broken up into three paratrooper training centers at Cercottes, Perpignan, and Roscanvel.

tion of Section 29. All in all I was considered an expert in dirty tricks and sabotage.

In Indochina I first served in the 1st RPC. The unit originally consisted of three battalions; however, the second battalion where I was serving had been so badly decimated that it had been broken up. The two remaining battalions were now stationed at Philippeville in Algeria and a 3rd paratrooper battalion of the Foreign Legion that only existed on paper had been added, which was the main reason I was so opposed to what had happened in Indochina. I had lost too many comrades at Dien Bien Phu and didn't want to see that happen again. Later, the 3rd battalion of the Foreign Legion was also broken up and on November 1, 1955 the two remaining battalions were merged into what became the 1st RCP. Because of all this reorganization the 1st RCP was now called the 41st Demi-Brigade Parachutiste and since I had been assigned to that unit, it was like a homecoming.

The ship was practically empty aside from about fifteen *gendarmes* and a handful of civilians. The second in command was replacing the captain of the ship who was ill with laryngitis after having screamed out his orders during a very stormy crossing coming over. We had dinner together, holding on to the table as best we could while the Mediterranean was going wild. The next day, once the sea had calmed down again and the coastline of Algeria appeared on the horizon, I remembered the happy days I had spent there just a few years before.

I had first served in Algeria in 1941 as an officer cadet. I had two Arab NCOs to assist me in a unit of Chahuhia native infantry from the Aurès Mountains. It was at a camp at Telerghma, a small base lost in the desert some 50 kilometers south of Constantine. I was happy there first of all because I was able to catch up on my studies and wrote a dissertation on "The Representation of the Supernatural in the works of Virgil," and because I was in one of the very last units of the French army on horseback. I must say that we did look pretty good on our Arabian horses. My horse was called *Babouin*.

One day we galloped back from a farmhouse with Captain Chrétien, an athlete who had been part of the French pentathlon team at the Berlin Olympics but nevertheless didn't stop falling off his horse. He had given me a basket full of eggs to hold on to, no doubt to test me. I had made it a point to not break any of the eggs. That kind of challenge symbolized just about my entire career. Captain Chrétien had a pretty fiancée and the eggs I didn't break were meant for her. Horses played an important part in my life more than once. My father had put me in the saddle at the age of eight and horseback riding was at the root of my choice of a military career. As an adolescent I looked down on the foot soldiers and wanted to be a cuirassier, just like the poet Lenau or a dragoon like my great-great uncle, Captain Soual, whose portrait hung in my room many years before in our big house in the Tarn. Captain Soual was a kind of family hero and I had built my own myth regarding his adventures that had taken him, just like me, to Algeria. Very proud of that ancestor, I took "Captain Soual" as my pseudonym inside the special services where everyone had to use a secret name.

I had learned Arabic at Telerghma, but I was unable to use it much in my unit because the men only spoke French and their own dialect. That tour of duty had only lasted one year. To become a regular army officer I had to attend the infantry school at Saint-Maixent, which by then had been moved to Aix-en-Provence.

The uneven Algerian coastline was drawing closer. After my experience in the *maquis* I couldn't help thinking that it must be easy for the rebels to have weapons delivered in small boats. French troops were very busy inside the country and were certainly too few to guard the coast. In any case that kind of surveillance duty would have been very boring and detrimental to army morale. While I looked from the bridge at the white town built up facing the sea, as the ship slowly entered the harbor, I thought back to my Algerian infantrymen. I was never to see them again, since my section had been wiped out during the campaign in Tunisia in May 1943, when the French army of Africa took the offensive alongside the Allies under Montgomery's command, defeating the German and Italian forces.

But the weather was beautiful and I could think only of those who were alive. I had many friends still living in Algeria. I was to find my old buddies from Indochina and a cousin of mine who worked at the treasury office of the city of Algiers. My family was also going to come over very soon.

2

Philippeville, 1955

A jeep was waiting at the pier to take me to brigade headquarters in a house located only half a kilometer from
the port area. The rest of the unit was accommodated in
scattered barracks in town and close to the airport where a
parachute jumping school had been set up.

When I reported to the dapper Colonel de Cockborne,
the commanding officer, he was very gracious in welcoming
me with a quasi-British flair. After listening to me with a
smile, perhaps because of my accent, which makes me sound
like a musketeer from Gascony, he came to the heart of the
matter:

"It's excellent that you come from the special services, because I'm in desperate need of an intelligence officer."

"I'm happy about that," I answered, with a smile of my own. "There's a problem, however."

"What's that?"

"You may have been misinformed because I'm not an intelligence specialist. I'm from the *Action Service*," I answered.

"I'm very much aware of your background and I'm sure you'll adapt very quickly. I guarantee that you'll see a lot of action because while the town looks quiet, the countryside is extremely restless. My battalions are in action right now."

"Where is this operation taking place, Colonel?"

"One is in the Aurès and the other at border with Tunisia."

The battalions of the brigade were actually in the field on specific operations against rebels who were attacking villages and isolated farms, looting, and killing the *pieds-noirs*. That was how I became an intelligence officer. It is an assignment that wasn't necessary in peacetime, and had not been reinstated by the commanding officer. I therefore had to restart the intelligence unit from scratch since the colonel had neither orders nor any files to give me.

During war, the mission of the intelligence officer is mainly to gather the information required to carry out operations, documentation centering on the enemy and the location in question. Those assignments are not to the liking of most officers and basically require a rather special kind of mindset, allowing the officer in charge to withstand the snide remarks of his colleagues. The success of the intelligence officer is also dependent upon the qualities of his commander and whether or not he shows much interest in intelligence work. Regimental commanders rarely display any real interest, and dispatching me to the unit was no picnic.

The driver took me in the jeep to my apartment, which was in one of the refurbished Adrian barracks, named after a quartermaster who had designed them as well as the blue helmet of the "poilus" of the First World War. Philippeville was a pretty little town of 21,000 and I quickly met the most important citizens. It began with some small-town pleasant-ries when I was invited to cocktails and dinner parties. Those first few days felt like a vacation under the African sun and beyond my workload I had enough free time to walk along the beach, read, listen to the radio and sometimes go to the movies. After a few weeks it became clear that my assign-ment was definitely no sinecure and my free time was quickly disappearing. On paper my task appeared to be a simple one but it was rather complicated because of the many fac-tors that went into it. I had to gather all possible informa-tion regarding the rebels from both military and civilian sources. There are two ways of getting information: either seeking it actively or waiting for it to come to you. As the weeks went by the rebellion grew in size, with time becom-ing more important and my role turning into a more aggres-sive one.

The government of Pierre Mendès-France had just been toppled by Parliament and his successor, Edgar Faure, had decided to quickly resolve the various problems of the Maghreb. That was the reason behind the decision taken in Paris to liquidate the FLN as fast as possible. There were additional reasons beyond strictly political requirements that were tied to the international situation, since the entire world seemed to be interested in the problem. To destroy the FLN required having the political will as well as the means to do so. The police force was not set up for such a task and the officers and NCOs of the regiments had not been trained for the kind of war where a traditional army must fight a rebellion that, in order to develop and grow, has to blend in with the civilian population and draw it into the struggle through terror and propaganda. The first step was to dispatch the clean-up teams, of which I was a part. Rebel leaders had to be identified, neutralized, and eliminated discreetly. By seeking information on FLN leaders I would automatically be able to capture the rebels and make them talk.

Philippeville was located in what was known as the North-Constantinois, the region where the FLN was strongest at the time. If there was to be a violent revolt in Algeria it was easy to forecast that it would start right there. Finding out how and when was our main problem and my job. In order to operate I needed a team. The colonel quickly assigned me two soldiers, Sergeant Kemal Issolah and Corporal Pierre Misiry. Issolah came from a prominent family of Turkish Janissaries that had been imported into the Kabylie by the Sultan of the Ottoman Empire, with the mission of keeping law and order in exchange for land and honorary titles. His family had joined the French side after the conquest of Algeria in 1830, and many of his ancestors had been officers and NCOs in the French army. Kemal's father was the latest and had retired with the rank of major in the colonial infantry. Kemal volunteered at the age of 18 following his military preparation courses, serving in Indochina as a corporal in a sniper unit. His battalion had been wiped out and Kemal was of the few remaining survivors.

Kemal volunteered once more in the paratroopers and was assigned to the 1st RCP as a sergeant. His knowledge of all Arab and Berber dialects spoken by the Muslims was very impressive. This extremely valuable man was clearly underemployed and the colonel had appointed him quarter-master, thinking that he wouldn't abscond with the money order funds because he was wealthy enough on his own account.

Pierre Misiry came from a French family, originally from the Ardèche region, that had immigrated to Tunisia and was therefore fluent in North African Arabic. He had also joined the army at 18 years of age and fought in the airborne in Indochina.

With the help of those two vigorous young men I suddenly felt very confident and began setting up my network.

I started by meeting everyone who could possibly be of any help, beginning with Captain Bastouil, who was the garrison chief in charge of military etiquette and ceremonies, such as parades and other exercises. He was an old para-trooper and told me that he issued a quarterly report and sought the help of the *Renseignements Généraux*, known as the RG. I had never worked with the police department before and couldn't tell what the differences were between the various branches. With Bastouil's help I quickly understood that the RG was in fact the intelligence unit of the local sub-prefecture. I then met with Police Superintendent Arnassan, who was in charge and suggested that I meet two of his colleagues, Superintendent Bourges, head of the criminal division, and Chief Superintendent Alexandre Filiberti, in charge of urban security. I developed close, friendly relations with those three officials, and worked with them on a daily basis.

There was also the *Gendarmerie*, and the unit I had the most important relations with was the research brigade led by Sergeant Major Buzonie, originally from Périgord in southern France; he didn't get along with his commanding officer but could take the initiative when necessary. Once they trusted me, the policemen told me in no uncertain terms the nature of what we were facing and the threats of attack that loomed over the little town. They made no mystery as to the methods they had to use and the ridiculously inadequate tools at their disposal. They quickly informed me that the best way to force a terrorist who refused to disclose what he knew was to torture him. They spoke in hushed voices but were not ashamed of using methods that everyone in the government back in Paris was well aware of and that some newspapers were beginning to discuss.

Before coming to Philippeville I had questioned prisoners from time to time but I had never used torture. I heard that such methods had been used in Indochina but only in extreme cases. In any event, it never happened in my battalion and most units serving in Algeria had never been faced with that problem before. I had killed men in the course of my profession and done things that severely tested my nerves but I never expected something like this. I often thought that I would be tortured someday but I had never reversed the problem and imagined that I would be torturing other people. In Morocco in 1942, right after I joined the secret services, Captain Delmas, an air force security officer, had found it necessary to warn me:

"Are you at least aware of what you're risking by volunteering for the special services?"

"Yes, Captain, I run the risk of being executed by firing squad."

"My poor boy," said Delmas rolling his eyes to the sky. "When they shoot you'll be relieved, because they will have tortured you first. And you'll realize that torture is much less fun than death!'"

In the Resistance and then inside the Service my friends told me that it was impossible to withstand torture and that a moment comes when you could talk, but were expected to hold out for at least 48 hours by screaming at the top of your lungs. Some torturers are even more fragile than their victims and can be impressed by your screams, and screaming helps you get through the pain. Those 48 hours allowed one's fellow agent or agents, who could be betrayed, some time to make plans. As a last resort you could use your poison capsule to end it all. I was mentally ready for every possible form of torture but I decided to never bring along the mandatory cyanide capsule on any of my missions. If they grabbed me I'd yell at first and after that we would see what happened.

Every time I would board a plane taking off at night I would think back to all that. I imagined being burned, my fingernails and teeth being torn out, like they had done to one of my buddies. Flying low over the English Channel those thoughts always came to haunt me when the American crew would pass around some whiskey and we would refuse. It was a kind of ritual. When anti-aircraft shelling started and the bursts of cannon fire would light up the sky we knew we were flying over the French coastline. The plane would climb up to 7,000 feet to avoid the shelling and no one said a word. I'd imagine the firing squad and decided to refuse to have my eyes covered. But then suddenly the hatch would open and there was only silence and the empty black sky.

The policemen at Philippeville, like all the other policemen in Algeria, were using torture and their commanding officers knew it. Those policemen were neither monsters nor tormentors, just ordinary men. They were certainly devoted to their country and deeply committed to duty but were swept up in extraordinary circumstances. I quickly became convinced that those circumstances explained and justified their methods. As surprising as it may appear, the use of this kind of violence, which is unacceptable under normal circumstances, could become inevitable in a situation that clearly defied every rule. The policemen had one guiding principle when they had to question a man who had shed innocent blood in the name of an ideal: torture was legitimate in cases when it was urgent to obtain information. If a lead was given in time scores of human lives could be saved. One idea had impressed me in particular. As I was sipping a glass of *pastis* and cautiously engaging in shoptalk with some of my colleagues, a policeman who had guessed that the issue of torture was bothering me said suddenly:

"Just think for a moment that you are personally opposed to torture as a matter of principle and that you have arrested a suspect who is clearly involved in preparing a violent attack. The suspect refuses to talk. You choose not to insist. Then the attack takes place and it's extremely bloody. What explanation will you give to the victim's parents, the parents of a child, for instance, whose body was torn to pieces by the bomb, to justify the fact that you didn't use every method available to force the suspect into talking?"

"I wouldn't like to face that problem," I answered.

"OK, but act as if you always expect to have to face it and then you'll see the difficulty: torture a suspected terrorist or tell the parents of the victims that it's better to let scores of innocent people be killed rather than make a single accomplice suffer."

That short discussion swept away any doubts I may still have harbored. I reached the conclusion that no one would ever have the right to pass judgment on our actions and that, should I have to do extremely unpleasant things in the course of my mission, I would never have any regrets.

Almost all the French soldiers who served in Algeria knew more or less that torture was being used but didn't question the methods because they didn't have to face the problem directly. A small minority engaged in it without being sorry they did, even though they found the practice disgusting. Most regular army officers never tortured anyone, simply because they were never placed in that kind of situation. As for the draftees, giving them that kind of assignment was completely out of the question. The people who opposed using torture were clearly FLN sympathizers and some bleeding heart idealists in metropolitan France or elsewhere who, had *they* been ordered to interrogate the terrorists, would have probably become among the most ruthless inquisitors.

I also met with other government officials besides the policemen, who, because of their position, might have important information I could use. For instance, an engineer named Bulle of the Water and Forest service. He ran a number of forest cabins scattered over the entire territory that were maintained by Muslims loyal to the French cause. Those cabins made up a valuable network to spread and acquire important information. I also had the assistance of a justice of the peace named Voglimacci, who came from the town of Cargese in Corsica where, he said, the Catholic religion had become very similar to Greek Orthodox religious rites. Colonel de Cockborne suggested that I meet Captain Ducay, who was in command of the parachute jumping school. That was finally someone I did know! Martial Ducay was a former riot policeman who had become a paratrooper and our paths had crossed in Indochina. I knew what an avid hunter he was. There was mostly wild boar and young partridge in the countryside around Philippeville and since it was rigorously forbidden to do any kind of hunting I suspected that Ducay was doing some poaching now and then.

After making all these contacts I very patiently started setting up my network, where each informer was a thread, including retailers, small business manufacturers, business-men, and lawyers, among others. I also found out how to use the local newspaperman, the owners of bistros, the lady who ran the nightclub, and even the madam at the whore-house. With the help of the mayor and town record keeper, Dominique Benquet-Crevaux, and one of his councilors, I created a file of the people living in the area.

I began gathering information on the FLN, its sympa-thizers and the members of the MNA. My system worked so well that I quickly had the names of suspects who were unquestionably tied to the bloodiest crimes. Upon their ar-rest it was obvious to me that these were not heroes but only brutal thugs. When I questioned them I started by ask-ing what they knew and they clearly indicated that they were not about to talk. Isn't someone accused of a crime natu rally inclined to either deny everything or to remain silent?

Then without any hesitation, the policemen showed me the technique used for "extreme" interrogations: first, a beat-ing, which in most cases was enough; then other means, such as electric shocks, known as the famous "gégène"; and finally water. Torture by electric shock was made possible by generators used to power field radio transmitters, which were extremely common in Algeria. Electrodes were attached to the prisoner's ears or testicles, then electric charges of varying intensity were turned on. This was apparently a well-known procedure and I assumed that the policemen at Philippeville had not invented it.

Fearing these methods or because of their use, the prisoners began providing very detailed explanations and even other names, allowing me to make further arrests. Since I had to take an active part with the police in these "extreme" interrogations, I thought it necessary to report back to Colonel de Cockborne, who became rather alarmed.

"Are you sure there aren't other ways of getting people to talk?" he asked me nervously. "I mean methods that are ..."

"Faster?" I asked.

"No, that's not what I mean."

"I know what you mean, Colonel. You're thinking of cleaner ways. You feel that none of this fits in with our humanistic tradition."

"Yes, that's what I mean," answered the Colonel.

"Even if I did agree with you, sir, to carry out the mission you've given me, I must avoid thinking in moral terms and only do what is most useful. As of now the rebellion is located for the most part in the countryside. Tomorrow it can hit the house next door."

"And how do you handle the suspects afterwards?" asked the Colonel.

"You mean once they've talked?"

"That's right."

"If they're connected to the crimes perpetrated by the terrorists, I shoot them."

"But you do understand that the bulk of the FLN is involved in terrorism!" answered de Cockborne.

"Yes, I know that."

"Wouldn't it be better to hand them over to the judicial system rather than execute them? We can't just go around knocking off every member of an organization! It's crazy!"

"But, Colonel, that's what the highest governmental authorities have decided. The courts don't want to handle the FLN precisely because there are too many of them, because we wouldn't know where to put them, and because we can't just send hundreds of people to the guillotine. The justice system is set up to handle a peacetime situation in metropolitan France. This is Algeria, where a war is about to start. You wanted an intelligence officer on your staff? You have one, Colonel. Since you gave me no orders I had to improvise. One thing is very clear: our mission demands results, requiring torture and summary executions, and as far as I can see it's only beginning."

"This is a dirty war and I don't like," he answered.

Colonel de Cockborne looked downcast because he knew I was right and I could sense that he would not remain in Algeria for very long.

Soon after that conversation I met with officers of the 2nd Bureau in Constantine under the command of Colonel Decomps. They asked me to gather information about cooperation between the PCA (Algerian Communist Party) and the FLN. There were some FLN military units organized under the name of ALN (National Liberation Army) but these didn't have any weapons and were desperately trying to obtain them. I was to find that out through an act of heroism that historians have decided to overlook, but that history will remember.

One day a group of rebels took over a forest cabin, which was guarded by Corporal Boughera Lakdar. He had a shotgun and when the head of the FLN group demanded that he hand it over the corporal refused:

"My gun belongs to France! If you want it, come and get it!" he cried out.

With those words the forest guard opened fire, killing the leader. Boughera Lakdar was taken and executed on the spot. There is no inscription on any monument that I know of bearing his name.

I found out about the incident from an eyewitness account that reached my network. It showed rather clearly that many Algerian Muslims were ready to sacrifice their lives for what they felt was their homeland.

Superintendent Bourges told me that our most bitter enemies were four nationalists who had escaped from prison in Bône in 1952 and had become among the most important leaders of the FLN. One of them was Zighoud Youssef, a former blacksmith from the little town of Condé-Smendou (which has since been renamed Zighoud Youssef), who at age 34 had been promoted FLN leader of the North-Constantine area. His predecessor was Didouche Mourad, whose group had been encircled and defeated by Colonel Ducourneau and his unit, the 18th RPC garrisoned at Saint-Charles, twenty kilometers from Philippeville. Didouche had been killed during the operation.

There was also a young man named Garsallah Messaoud, age 23, whose picture we had and who looked like the actor Alain Delon. Since he wasn't very tall, and because of his youthful good looks, he was nicknamed Little Messaoud. He had been a Muslim Boy Scout, which hadn't stopped him from being professionally unemployed and then turning into a small-time crook. At the start of the war he divided his time between little scams and pimping. But he was ambitious, strong, totally merciless, and typical of a certain breed of rebel. The FLN had allowed him to acquire a bit of glory, as it did for many others with nothing to lose. Because of his openly proclaimed indifference to human life he had built a reputation for himself and was clearly a brave man. The day we caught up with him there was no doubt in my mind that he would give us a lot of trouble.

Little Messaoud had attracted a group of young fanatics around him. Along the airport at Philippeville there was a cliff overhanging the runway by about 250 feet. Superintendent Bourges told me that Messaoud's men had an observation post on top of the cliff. It was an impregnable position and bombing would have been useless in those rocks. Police Inspector Jeannot di Meglio found out that Little Messaoud's group had managed to recruit one of his informers. The informer, about 40 years old and rather likable, was a small-time thief and a fence for stolen automobile tires. He admitted to Jeannot that he feared having to do battle with the paratroopers in a firefight and asked to be held as a prisoner, hoping to remain in custody for two years, which he considered a safer place to be. At Bourges' request I went to see Judge Voglimacci, who refused to place the informer under arrest without a motive, since the man hadn't volunteered into the FLN and had never taken part in any armed or terrorist act. There was nothing we could do, so we had a meeting—the little crook, Jeannot di Meglio, Bourges, and myself. We placed him under arrest as he had requested and then found him a job as a driver. Shortly thereafter he lost his head and began blackmailing his former FLN friends. In the fall of 1956 they slit his throat.

I was meeting a lot of people. Not all of them upstanding citizens but they found working with me to be in their best interests. I had several of these informers infiltrate the underground, which proved to be a more effective method than using those who were already inside. Issolah had infiltrated the FLN. At night he would slip into some blue workmen's overalls and have coffee with the rebels. He even brought a disbelieving NCO with him once, saying that the blond young man was a Kabyle who understood no Arabic.

I was working extremely hard and, thankfully, most of the time I didn't need to resort to torture, but only talk with people. Many such conversations were friendly and for our public relations we used everything we had, even our supplies of bullets. The French army had a problem at that time in acquiring quality weapons and many soldiers were even forced to buy them in ordinary gun shops; however, we did have as much ammunition as we needed. Training sessions were held regularly and the supply depot gave us large quantities of bullets, more in fact than we could use. The NCOs had large supplies and passed some of them along to their friends in the police department. The policemen were not the only ones to ask for more bullets. The *pieds-noirs* had also armed themselves and needed bullets too. The manager of the supply depot, a master sergeant from Corsica who had no qualms, came to see me directly:

"Captain, ammunition is scarce for the good people. They ask me for it but I can't give it to them. If you could set up a bogus firing exercise and let me have a few crates I can guarantee you that I will put them to good use."

"And who will you give them to?"

"To my fellow citizens in Philippeville, naturally!"

Denunciations began flowing in. There were many small villages in the countryside that were opposed to the FLN in principle. Besides the desire to live in peace there were also old rivalries and private resentments involving women for the most part. Naturally, whenever I acquired any information that would increase the hostility of the Algerian Muslims toward the FLN I didn't hesitate to use it. It was also a common occurrence for the rebels to denounce each other.

3

June 18th

Whardn it launched the insurrection in November 1954, the FLN had failed to massively draw the population in its wake, as it had hoped. Contrary to what many people believed, the rebellion had not spread like wildfire and one could even say that by the spring of 1955 it was running out of steam. Therefore the FLN radically switched tactics. From now on the rebellion would make systematic use of terrorism, targeting the civilian population, whether it was Algerian Muslims who were known to be "friendly" to France, or Europeans. The FLN could easily intimidate the countryside but was having difficulty organizing itself within urban areas. That was precisely where terrorism was going to develop.

During the spring of 1955, after several months of taking a wait-and-see attitude that was encouraged by political instability, the government finally understood how much the situation was deteriorating. Urban guerrilla warfare had to be avoided at all costs. The new government with Edgar Faure as prime minister, which included Maurice Bourgès-Maunoury as interior minister, replacing François Mitterrand, and Robert Schuman as justice minister, decided to counter attack. On April 3 Parliament approved a state of emergency law allowing tighter cooperation between the police and military intelligence. It was a way of institutionalizing what I was already putting into practice unofficially in the field. From now on police and military operations were to be carried out in tight coordination.

During the days that followed a state of emergency was declared in the areas that had been most affected by the FLN. Everyone feared that things would get worse during Ramadan, which was to take place in May that year; in fact there was an increase in attacks at that time. A governmental committee decided in the middle of May to beef up military involvement and increase French troops from 60,000 to 100,000 men in Algeria. Drastic instructions were issued to make sure the rebellion was crushed, even authorizing bombing from the air, which the government until then had opposed. At the same time Paris secretly decided to liquidate all FLN leaders by any means available, including through the use of the special services.

Colonel de Cockborne had just been appointed military attaché to Rome, which was much better for everyone. I assumed that he had foreseen the kind of extreme measures we would be required to use and he didn't wish to participate in the beginnings of that operation. Colonel George Mayer, his deputy, replaced him. Mayer was a tough fair-haired man, nicknamed "Prosper" because of his rumored popularity with the ladies. His wife, the pretty Simone, came from a French family established in Morocco and she didn't seem to mind his reputation. She was known as "Monette."

Mayer was one of the oldest paratroopers in the French army and that added a lot of prestige to his good looks. He had volunteered right after graduating from Saint-Cyr, before the war, to be part of one of the two companies of the new units of airborne infantry that had been created in 1937 and had seen action during the campaign of France in the Alsace and Vosges regions. He had later served in Indochina. I felt he would be less strict than his predecessor as to the means required to defeat the FLN.

On June 18, 1955 a series of terrorist incidents took place in Philippeville. I saw this wave of unforeseen attacks as a personal insult and a provocation. I had been part of the special services of the Free French that belonged to the Big One's—as we nicknamed General Charles de Gaulle—personal staff. Therefore any incidents on a date like June 18 were unacceptable.* Furthermore, I was an intelligence officer now and I had uncovered no hints announcing the

---

* June 18, 1940 was the date of General de Gaulle's broadcast from London, appealing to the French people and the army to reject both the armistice with Germany and Marshal Pétain. De Gaulle was known as "The Man of June 18"—a date considered sacred by most Frenchmen. [Ed.]

incidents that had just taken place. And for an intelligence officer any surprise is extremely humiliating.

Seven bombs had exploded in different sections of town at the same time. Isolated groups had shot at European passers-by and also attacked them with sticks and knives. Some cars had been set on fire as well as a few storefronts. The police force, the gendarmerie, and the brigade had the situation under control rather quickly after some heavy fighting. An Algerian Muslim had approached a *pied-noir* who was walking in the street. They knew each other well and yet the Algerian split the man's head in two with an ax. Alexandre Filiberti, head of urban security, went to the bedside of the dying man, who whispered the name of his aggressor. I was given the information and we were able to arrest the Algerian almost immediately and start questioning him. I had to find out whether an organization had coordinated these attacks and if so who its leaders were.

It was important that he talk because we had been surprised by this wave of violence. Incidents of that kind could take place at any moment all over again, God only knew where, with more bombs exploding the next day. The most revolting part was that they had attacked only civilians and I had to find out who could have issued such orders. The man refused to talk and I decided to use violent methods. I did the job without the policemen. It was the first time that I tortured anyone. But it was useless that day because the man died without talking.

I didn't have any thoughts, nor did I regret his death. If I had any regrets at all it was that he hadn't talked before dying. He had used violence on someone who was not his enemy. It was someone whose only crime was to be there at the time. I could have understood had he picked an official, even a military man. But just anybody from Philippeville at random and someone he knew well on top of it? I felt neither hatred nor pity. Time was of the essence and I was looking at someone who was directly implicated in a terrorist act: any methods were good enough to force him to talk. That was what the circumstances demanded. After the prisoner's death, I asked my informers what was going on inside Philippeville. Had an armed group set itself up in town? I was finally able to find out that the real leaders were hiding in the countryside, in the rocky landscape, amid the shrubs and the caves. It was impossible to detect anything from a plane and rockets, bombs or even artillery wouldn't work to get them out.

At the beginning of July 1955, just as General Lorillot took over as commander-in-chief of all French forces in Algeria, the Oran sector was quiet and terror had almost stopped in the Algiers region where the FLN was making only a few isolated attacks. Only the Aurès Mountains and the area around Constantine remained difficult. Since it happened to be the area where the FLN was strongest it kept feeding a climate of terror and fear designed to bring about repression and force the uncommitted mass of the population to take its side. Around July 20 I became convinced that there was a large concentration of rebels in the wooded areas around Philippeville that were hard to reach. There were about 3,000 to 5,000 men, including *fellagha* fighters and civilians mixed together. Some of them were from the immediate areas around Philippeville, others were from the surrounding administrative departments. I activated my network and made a number of connections, a long and painstaking task.

Logically the rebels needed food and they were isolated. They had no supplies being parachuted in to them or any convoys coming from the outside. Therefore they had to get their food from Philippeville. With the help of the local police force I took a tour of the small food stores. Mohammed, the grocer from the Mzab region, who normally sold one sack of semolina every three days, had just sold fifty sacks in one shot. That was odd. But there was something even more disturbing: a man had gone into a pharmacy and purchased scores of bandages. I figured out through the analysis of information I had gathered that on August 20, 1955, at noon, the FLN was going to launch a massive frontal attack with several thousand men against Philippeville.

Zighoud Youssef was the head of the northern Constantine area and had decided to stage a spectacular and bloody attack on the anniversary of the deposition of Mohammed V, the Sultan of Morocco. Since 1952 Mohammed V had asked the President of France, Vincent Auriol, for a revision of the French protectorate of 1912, but this only led to the Sultan's removal and replacement by his uncle on August 20, 1953. The Sultan was sent off into exile to the island of Madagascar. Youssef also wanted to use the attack as a signal to support a motion at the United Nations by seven African and Asian countries, which included India, in favor of Algerian independence. The attack was also to be followed by commando action, where the men were to take up positions in the cellars of buildings all over town a few days before the offensive. The FLN high command wanted to take an entire Algerian mid-sized town as hostage.

I would find out later on that at the same time, on the same day, they also wanted to take over a town in Morocco. They chose Oued Zem, in order to demonstrate to the world that the nationalist movements of the Maghreb were acting in unison and could coordinate their actions. The rebels in Algeria did not have the power to take over a sizable town of any kind and could not take part in a general attack. Therefore to target Philippeville was a good solution. It was an active port city and the matter would certainly be noticed worldwide. And so I knew one month before it was to take place, the location, the date and the hour of the planned operation, including the number of men involved and the tactics that had been chosen. Now we had to sit tight and make no moves while we dug in, waiting for the enemy.

4

The Attack

I informed Colonel Mayer and traveled to Constantine to also inform Colonel Decomps of the 2nd Bureau.

"Colonel, it's quite simple: we will be attacked in Philippeville on August 20."

"Have you found out anything about a similar operation against Constantine?"

"They only discussed Philippeville. I have no information regarding the Constantine region," I answered.

"And above us, in Algiers? Do you think something will happen there?"

"No, nothing will take place above us—at least not right away. The FLN isn't ready for a general offensive."

I returned to Philippeville and wrote a report, which I handed in to the Colonel.

"Your report is all well and good," said Mayer, "but now it must be signed and passed along."

"Sign it and send it," I answered.

Mayer was hesitating:

"What if nothing happens on August 20? What will I look like? Do you actually believe I'm about to take that kind of a chance?"

"But Colonel," I was suddenly yelling at him, "I tell you something *will* happen! Come on and sign it now! Goddamn shit!"

In my excitement I had used the favorite curse word of the Big One. Maybe that's what convinced Prosper. In any case he grabbed his pen and signed my report without uttering another word.

On Thursday August 18, I was told that FLN commandos were beginning to take positions in the cellars around town. Obviously there was no way we were going to step in; it would only prove that we had sources of information. It was very hard to live with the knowledge that there were hundreds of men so close to us primed to kill. We were also very few and the next day I took a tally: our 1st Battalion had just returned from operations and the trainees from the paratrooper school would be used as additional forces. All told we had a total force of 400 excellent men, but 400 against several thousand made it a very tough challenge. Prosper had provided me with a deputy for this operation, Lieutenant Soutiras, a graduate of Saint-Cyr. He was a signals officer but hated the specialty and didn't mince his words in saying so. His father was a regular army officer, who had been killed fighting the Germans during the campaign of France in 1944.

The colonel gathered his officers on August 19. He didn't want to contradict me but I could sense that he didn't believe a single word of my forecasts. He read the report to the others, then turned to me:

"Tomorrow is Saturday and I must hand out graduation certificates at the paratrooper school in the morning. After that there will be a meeting at the trainers club. Do you suggest that I go there or not?"

"You should go," I replied. "The best thing to do is not change anything to your planned schedule because they could get suspicious."

"What do you suggest?"

"Nothing different, normal service, but by 11:55 a.m. everyone must be at his station, with weapons at the ready."

"Very well, gentlemen. Issue your orders: should the attack take place at noon, as we expect, fire at will until you finish your ammunition. Fire the machine guns without stopping. I'll call in reinforcements. Once the frontal attack has been stemmed, go around and take care of the commandos hiding in the cellars. And don't let them off the hook!"

On Saturday, August 20, 1955, I decided to go parachute jumping just for relaxation. I had to go very early because the wind would start blowing toward the sea at dawn and the jump area was on the coastline. I woke up at 3 a.m. and after jumping I returned to the brigade barracks at daybreak. Across the street there was a café owned by the son-in-law of the mayor of Philippeville. At 8 a.m. I quietly crossed the street to have a big breakfast with some very strong coffee, fried eggs and wine. I knew that the commandos were watching me from their cellars and were dying to shoot at me. The heat was already stifling at that hour. A police inspector dropped by.

"So, Captain, are you ready?" he asked.

"Right now as you can see I'm enjoying breakfast. You can't fight well on an empty stomach."

"A taxi driver has just informed me that his car has been requisitioned by the FLN."

A second fellow came into the bistro saying that there wasn't a single taxi at the railroad station. We all suddenly thought about the taxis of the Marne. Colonel Mayer was friendly with Paul Ducourneau, who had graduated from Saint-Cyr in the same class and was in command of the 18th RCP in Saint-Charles. Ducourneau said that nothing was expected in his sector. If the attack did take place he promised to come to our rescue as fast as he could. His second battalion was stationed some six kilometers south of Philippeville. The FLN was able to listen in to both the radio and the phone lines. We agreed to signal Captain Thomas, who was in command of the second battalion.

"Don't worry, Georges," Ducourneau had said. "Should the *fellagha* show up, just ring and Thomas will come around with the 18/2 to kick some ass."

Now it was almost noon. I was giving my final orders to the men when Superintendent Filiberti, the deputy police commissioner in charge of public safety, arrived with two policemen.

"Captain, I urgently need you to lend me some men and your Dodge."

"What for?"

"Well, two of my policemen have to go to the Roman quarry and make an arrest."

The Roman quarry was located 2 kilometers south of Philippeville, very close to the place where the 2nd Battalion of the 18th RCP was stationed.

"I'm sorry to tell you, Inspector, that I can't do it."

"And why is that?"

"You're asking me why? The *fellagha* are getting ready to attack Philippeville less than one hour from now!"

"But we'll be done in less than an hour. I can guarantee it."

"Filiberti," I said, "this is no time to go moseying around over there with them all worked up and getting killed in the process."

"But it'll take us less than two minutes. You can't refuse me that!"

I called in Issolah and Misiry.

"Escort these gentlemen to the Roman quarry, collar the guys, and come back at top speed. And, naturally, don't get into a firefight! That's an order."

Half an hour later Filiberti came back, looking downcast.

"Bad news. I got a call from the CRS station south of Philippeville. Our men have been stopped by at least 500 *fellagha*."

"Well, shit! I knew that was a stupid thing to do, going down there. I won't send anyone else."

"So, what do we do?"

"You got them into this mess. You get them out of it!"

Filiberti ran over to his car and came back with his 24-29 automatic machine gun that he had brought from his office and that he always kept at hand.

"I'm going to get them!"

"Going from bad to worse," I told him. "We've already lost four men and if we throw in the inspector we're getting off to a great start!"

Filiberti went off anyway. When he reached the area with his men they saw Issolah, Misiry, and the other two defending themselves desperately against a wave of *fellagha*, along with a group of chanting women. Filiberti got out of his car and began shooting at them with his automatic rifle. There was a truck a few hundred meters away giving off a heavy smell of gasoline: it was carrying Molotov cocktails to be used for the attack on Philippeville. Issolah took advantage of the arrival of the inspector and his men to throw a grenade up close, setting off a thunderous explosion. They succeeded in falling back and when they returned it was about 11:30 a.m.

"So when is your party going to start?" asked Prosper sarcastically.

"It's already started, Colonel, and I think it's time to call in the 18/2 because we're going to have a hell of a fight."

We asked the Thomas battalion to head for the Roman quarry, where the rebels had wasted time because of that skirmish. They had some dead and were taking time to rescue the wounded. The Thomas battalion had to travel only 4 kilometers to intercept them, a very short distance to run for paratroopers in good training condition. The 18/2 got into the fight and began shooting into the group without holding back. The chanting women did not impress the paratroopers and anyone standing in the way was mowed down and killed. Unfortunately there were women and children that the *fellagha* had dragged along with them.

At noon, in downtown Philippeville, shooting began from all sides. The rebels were farmers who had been given rudimentary weapons and were led by FLN militants who were much better equipped. The impressive part was that they advanced along the streets, marching as if they were on the parade ground. Philippeville was a town of 20,000 and even though many of its citizens were at the beach the whole story could take a very ugly turn. Then, in unison, the commandos, who had been lurking for three days in the cellars, took to the streets. The brigade countered them immediately. Our headquarters, where I was located, came under fire by individuals emerging from a bistro-hotel across the street, just next to the one I usually patronized. They attacked, screaming at the top of their lungs.

I was fed up very quickly with all that noise and took to the street with some of my men. The assailants were surprised to see us and to be suddenly under the fire of our submachine guns. They quickly fell back into the bistro but continued to shoot. We ran across the square, doubling up under a hail of bullets that whizzed around our ears. We were now under an infernal crossfire from the buildings in front and the rebels coming into the streets. It was looking more and more like hell on earth. The café had a main door and a rear exit door. I yelled at Misiry to follow me to try and smoke the rebels out with grenades by getting in through the back door. But it was locked shut. Misiry shot up the keyhole with his submachine gun and we could see how thick the door was from the impact of the shells. Some shots must have gotten through because we heard screaming from inside.

We ran back to the bistro's main entrance and were welcomed by a heavy round of gunfire. After throwing a few grenades inside we stormed the main room, spraying it with several rounds of machine gun fire. I never saw so many broken bottles and I am even not mentioning the owner, who should never have decided to stay behind the counter. The rebels ran back down into the cellars but didn't lock themselves in and continued shooting from the open door, determined as they were to hold out, come what may. We couldn't get near them and it was impossible to finish them off without heavy losses. I ordered my men not to attempt any heroics and to just keep on shooting as a diversion. Meantime, with Misiry we got as close as we could and threw in two grenades. Once they exploded a fire broke out.

The shooting stopped but the cellar was big and I knew the commandos were still hiding inside and would soon make a sortie. On both sides we stopped breathing and loaded new clips in our machine guns. Suddenly about twenty men sprang forward from the smoking cellar. We were waiting for them with our submachine guns and not one of them survived.

The battle was raging outside. We went to Communist Party headquarters. The party members had cautiously left the premises and had been replaced by about fifty FLN rebels who had spent the night there. The proof of collusion on the part of the Communist Party and the FLN that Lieutenant Colonel Decomps of the 2nd Bureau in Constantine had requested was absolutely indisputable. In the street next to the brigade barracks, the rebels continued to advance, looking hallucinated. I found a legionnaire who was hanging around to help me stop them. He began shooting at the men with his rifle and they fell, one after the other. But I could not understand their behavior. When a *fellagha* was hit and fell to the ground his comrades didn't even react; they just kept on coming forward, displaying total indifference instead of taking cover or turning around. They didn't appear concerned by what was happening. In the streets nearby they were welcomed with heavy machine gun fire, yet none of these men fell back and they therefore suffered enormous losses.

Deputy Prefect Dupuch had cabled Algiers in a panic, saying that Philippeville had fallen to the FLN and that it was all over. Then he locked himself up in his cellar. But on a Saturday in Algiers everyone was at the beach and they paid no more attention to Dupuch's messages than to Mayer's report, which had been sent in two months before. No one had taken seriously the threats hanging over us. I knew this through a cousin of mine who was living in Algiers and whom I visited occasionally. His friends were saying that the FLN didn't exist.

The rebels lost 134 dead in the streets of Philippeville and several hundred wounded, whom they didn't even attempt to rescue. The brigade had to pick them up and an NCO was shot as he tried to bring back a wounded *fellagha*. One of our squad leaders had been shot at from a cellar. Rather than set fire to the building or force them out with hand grenades, he decided to attack the rebels fairly and paid the supreme price for his foolishness. Two men had lost their lives trying to play by the rules, in addition to about another 100 wounded on our side as well.

We picked up a rather battered minor FLN leader on the ground in front of the police station he had tried to attack. That had been a bad idea because Filiberti was waiting for him with his 24-29 automatic rifle. All the rebels who were part of that leader's squad had been killed and he was unlucky enough to be on file with Filiberti. The police superintendent was in no special hurry to get the man to the hospital and wanted to question him instead. He requested the help of Issolah, who played the role of being another FLN prisoner and was brutally thrown into the wounded prisoner's cell.

"We've been unlucky," sniveled Issolah, who was also a very good actor. "We really got clobbered today."

"Yes," the FLN leader answered, "but Zighoud Youssef, the leader of the Constantine region, survived, as well as Si Khaled."

"Si Khaled? Who's that?"

"Si Khaled… El Mesri."

The prisoner then suddenly died. Another FLN leader had been seriously wounded in the thigh by a burst of heavy machine gun fire. Doctor Vincent, the surgeon at the Philippeville hospital, operated on him with the assistance of Doctor Py, who had come in from Algiers. They couldn't get him properly anesthetized because the anesthetic the nurse had given to him by injection didn't work. A second injection was necessary. As soon as the operation was finished the rebel opened his eyes and the surgeons understood: most of the assailants had been drugged silly with the "kif" they had smoked, which explained why they had been so indifferent when we were shooting at them.

By 1 p.m. it was all over. Following Zighoud Youssef's orders, the leaders, seeing things were going badly, had decided to pick up the weapons of the dead and fall back, leaving their men behind, whether they were still standing or wounded, to face us alone. Youssef had figured out precisely the heavy losses he would incur because the fighters had only light weapons. The objective was to make an impact on public opinion: the more blood there was the more they would talk about it. Youssef had sent some farmers out in front, doped up with hashish. Clearly their death meant nothing to him, not much more than the death of the French civilians he had ordered them to massacre. I understood that without my intelligence information, there would have been a massacre at Philippeville, similar to the atrocities at El Halia.

5

El-Halia

Around 2 p.m. we were told that the attack concentrating on Philippeville also involved a few villages and small towns near Constantine. There was an isolated iron sulphur mine some 22 kilometers to the east and the FLN had targeted it for an attack. At El-Halia some 2,000 Algerian Muslims lived side by side with 130 Europeans. All of them were paid according to the same salary scale and had identical social and health benefits, precisely the kind of situation the FLN couldn't accept. I never thought the rebels would attack the mine or that they would be so cowardly as to target only the civilians of European origin.

Zighoud Youssef had ordered all the European civilians to be killed and to kill them in the cruelest way possible. He expected that the French would react to this massacre, that they would be surprised by such terror, and start a mindless repression that would bring together the Algerian Muslim population against the *pieds-noirs* and stir up international public opinion. In the intense midday heat, while people were having lunch, two groups of *fellagha* had launched a surprise attack and began killing all the civilians who were inside their homes. There were small children inside the houses who were being kept out of the heat to avoid sunstroke and women who were quietly busy with the midday lunch as they waited for their husbands to come home.

I had visited the mine a few days before and checked the efficient self-defense system that the director had set up. Since relations between the French and the Algerian Muslims were excellent at El-Halia, I wasn't worried. The *pied-noir* employees felt very confident about their Algerian co-workers and were convinced that the fraternal feelings they shared would come into play should an attack take place. In order to avoid the risk of showing the FLN our hand, which would have delayed the attack and exposed my informers, making a later operation much more difficult to forecast, I didn't share any information with the director of the mine. As a cautionary measure I placed the Péhau military camp used for the training of young recruits, located ten kilometers away on the road to Philippeville, on the alert.

The defensive system at El-Halia was made up mostly of a good supply of rifles and submachine guns. And yet on the day of the attack the system didn't work because the man who had the key to the weapons supply location had gone off to the beach at Philippeville. Two European workers at the mine were able to slip away, reaching Camp Péhau, distraught and out of breath. They were crying and said that the men were killing with unbelievable ferocity, taking small children and crushing them to death against the walls and disemboweling women of every age after having raped them.

At Péhau we only had 200 young recruits under the command of Captain Perret, who had survived Dien Bien Phu, and Lieutenant Nectoux, who was originally from Burgundy. Once informed of the disaster, Mayer decided to take back the mine as soon as possible. To use green recruits who hadn't even finished their basic training and could barely reload their rifles or understand an order was extremely risky. However, they happened to be on the spot and Mayer was one to take on responsibility when it came down to it. He therefore gave Perret the order to attack without maneuvering, just like the soldiers of the French Revolution and in the simplest manner possible: on a line, shoulder to shoulder, and only open fire on command to avoid any accidents.

The only thing Mayer could do was to call in the tactical air force group from Constantine. Two T6, single engine training planes in use in Algeria for ground attack took off immediately to support the 200 recruits who unhesitatingly went on the offensive to save those civilians who were still alive. None of those boys panicked and they opened fire only on sight and when their officers gave the order. The pilots also did their job well and we counted 80 dead *fellagha* and some 60 prisoners. Unfortunately what they had had the time to do to the Europeans at the mine was beyond description. We found 35 bodies, 15 wounded and 2 persons were missing. When I saw children chopped up into pieces, with their throats slit or crushed to death, the women who had been disemboweled or decapitated, I think I really forgot what having any pity meant. What was hardest to believe was that these people had been massacred and mutilated by their Algerian Muslim neighbors, who had been peacefully living with them until then. The FLN had them drink alcohol and smoke "kif," then they had encouraged them to plunder the homes of the *pied-noir* workers and had showed them how to do it.

Towards 4 p.m. Nectoux phoned Mayer:

"Colonel, I'm up here at the mine and it's not a pretty sight, sir."

"Approximately how many?"

"Thirty, maybe forty, Colonel, but in such awful condition."

"Do you have any prisoners?"

"Yes, about sixty. What should I do with them, Colonel?"

"What a question! Get rid of them, naturally!"

Fifteen minutes later we heard GMC trucks pulling up with Nectoux.

"Why all these trucks, Nectoux?"

"Well, I brought the prisoners, Colonel, as I thought you meant."

Prosper and I tried not to laugh but felt we enraged inside. I said to Nectoux:

"Is it because you're from Burgundy that you don't understand the French language?"

The lieutenant felt hurt because he didn't like people making fun of his accent and he looked so miffed that we really began laughing like during those odd moments when tragedy suddenly seems grotesque.

"OK, Nectoux, unload your trucks and get out of here."

I told the colonel that I would take care of the job. Mayer didn't answer me, but we got along very well and I knew that he approved of what I was about to do. I picked one man among the prisoners to question him myself. He was an Algerian Muslim foreman who had murdered the entire family of one of his French co-workers.

"But why did you kill them, goddamn shit? They hadn't done anything to hurt you! How could you murder small babies?"

"I was told that I ran no risk."

"What do you mean you ran no risk? How could that be?"

"Yesterday an FLN representative came to see us. He told us the Egyptians and the Americans were landing today to come and help us. He said we should kill all the French and that we ran no risk. So I killed all those I could find."

I answered him in Arabic:

"I don't know what Allah thinks about what you've just done, but now you'll go and explain to him directly. Since you've murdered innocent people, you must also die. It's the rule of the paratroopers."

I called Issolah over.

"Take him away. He must be executed immediately! For the others I need to talk with Bébé."

"You mean Bébé the mechanic?"

"That's right."

Bébé had been a sergeant in the Resistance movement and his nickname came from his young-looking face. He was in charge of the motor pool. Since everyone knew what we were doing Bébé had come to see me a few days before.

"Captain, I need to talk to you."

"Go right ahead, Bébé."

"Look, I know what you're doing and I'd like to work with you."

"Sorry, Bébé, but I have all the men I need and I think we need you in the garage." He was disappointed but kept on asking anyway.

"Captain, if some day you need help, don't forget I'm here."

"It's a deal. I won't forget."

On August 20 I remembered Bébé's offer.

"If I recall correctly you said you knew what my job was," I said, "and wanted to work with me."

"That's right, Captain."

"Well, I accept your offer and today I do have a job for you. Go get all your men with their submachine guns and all the loaded clips you can find."

I lined up the prisoners, both *fellagha* and the Algerian Muslim workers who had helped them. When the time came to fire, Bébé was clearly not very enthusiastic. I'm sure he would have much preferred being back in his grease pit. I had to give the orders myself. I was totally indifferent: we had to kill them and I did it. That was all. We purposely made it look as though we were abandoning the mine and some *pied-noir* survivors were left behind to stand guard. A few days later, as we expected, the *fellagha* returned. Once the guards gave us the signal we went up with the first battalion. We captured some 100 men, who were executed on the spot.

I ordered other executions following the battle of Philippeville. We captured some 1,500 rebels on the same day or the day after and we assembled them in a large courtyard. I came in with the policemen to sort them out. The law enforcement agencies, the RG, the urban Sûreté, the criminal police, and the Gendarmerie, were all there to take those they wanted to question. Among the prisoners were men from the mountains and farmers who had been forced into the FLN. We often recognized them and they were quickly set free. But there were others, the diehards, those who were ready to start all over again the next day if they were ordered to do so. How should we handle them once they had been questioned and had told us everything they knew? I had tried to sort them out into the various units that handled the interrogations, but once that was done, knowing that these men couldn't be rehabilitated, they were handed back to me so that I would take care of them. I wasn't told in so many words but the meaning was unmistakably clear. However, I didn't want to be responsible for the fate of so many prisoners and said so, strenuously:

"Please, Superintendent, his man should be under your supervision. Take him!"

"Can't you hold him for now?" he asked "I'll come back tomorrow morning to pick him up."

"My dear Superintendent, I'm really having a hard time, and I don't know where to put them. And what about you in the Gendarmerie?"

"I can't take him down to the barracks; there's no more room," he answered.

"You guys are really pissing me off now, all of you!"

I started all over again the next day but they were still just as evasive.

"And today do you want them? Yes or no, damn it?"

All the civilians were looking down at their shoes.

"OK, I get it."

I picked a few groups of NCOs and ordered them to shoot the prisoners. I was always careful not to order the same men to do that kind of work, and very rarely were they recruits, except for those who had seen action and had been in the army for at least one year. They didn't have any qualms.

Once it was over I prepared a report and helped the inspectors of the RG write theirs. Police Superintendent Arnassan was in France and I sat in his office. I found out that more massacres had taken place at El-Arushi, Oued Zenatti, Catinat, and Jemmapes. In Constantine a nephew of Ferhat Abbas had been murdered in his drugstore because he was thought to be too pro-French. We picked up the FLN members who had been killed in the uprising and took the bodies to the municipal stadium. There were 134 dead lined up on one of the tracks of the stadium, guarded by the soldiers of the 18th battalion. We found those who had dropped between the bushes a few days later because of the August heat.

The FLN had lost about 500 men, including those who had attacked the forts defending Philippeville and who had walked into machinegun fire. The local newspaperman had come around to take a look at the stadium and having bribed the sentry on duty he managed to get in and take some pictures, even moving some of the bodies around for a better angle. The photographs were then sold for their weight in gold to *Life* magazine so that those 135 dead became, thanks to the American press commentary, as many poor prisoners who had been executed by French paratroopers. The picture was doctored but the press wanted any kind of photo proving that we were just a bunch of bastards.

I asked the municipal services of Philippeville to place the funeral parlor at my disposal and to indicate where the Muslim cemetery was located. We had to dig a ditch in such a way that the bodies could lie in the direction of Mecca. In August the ground is as hard as rock so we needed a caterpillar shovel. The only one available was at the agricultural school. I went to talk to the principal with Soutiras, Issolah, Misiry, and two other *pieds-noirs*, Maurice Jacquet and Yves Cuomo, both of them corporals, chauffeurs, and mechanics. They could speak fluent Arabic. The principal of the school was a reserve officer yet he refused to lend us his shovel. I had to threaten him with arrest to get him to comply. We dug a ditch about 100 meters long, two meters wide and no more than one meter deep. We buried the bodies in that ditch.

The next day a woman from the health department of the Prefecture came to see me in my office. She represented the authorities in Algiers who were sending me lime to be sure the bodies would disappear. The same day we got an official message from the military command, also in Algiers, with orders to stop the repressive measures. However, through a different channel, I also got a discreet message of congratulations from the "dairy" and from Lefort, who had replaced me as instructor of the *Action Service*.

General Jacques Massu phoned Mayer on Monday, August 22, 1955, to announce his visit. Massu wanted to take advantage of the recent events to also inspect our unit. He was nominally in command of the 10th Paratrooper Division, which was still not fully operational. In less than one year of war Massu hadn't had the time to get to know the units under his command and he was astonished that in such a bloody fight our side had suffered only two dead soldiers.

He had lunch at the mess and as he was getting back into his helicopter he asked the question that had been on his mind:

"So, Mayer, tell me what happened here, because there's something I still don't understand about this matter."

"Well it's quite simple, General. We knew exactly when the attack was going to take place. You should ask Captain Aussaresses, the intelligence officer, that question."

"And who is he?"

"A special services officer who was sent to us and who was a paratrooper with the Free French."

Massu called me over.

"How the hell did you get that information?"

"I took the necessary steps and got help."

"From whom?"

"Well, from the police force among others."

Massu grunted and climbed into his helicopter without saying another word. I didn't suspect that he had me in his sights that day. Later we received a message from General Lorillot, supreme commander of the French army in Algeria. He wished to meet those officers who were candidates for promotion; however, none of us was promoted. There was no reward for any of the men in the brigade. We had saved thousands of civilians from a horrible fate but suddenly the French Republic didn't want to acknowledge us at all.

Brigitte Friang, a former member of the special services who had become a news reporter, came over to write an article. She was already friendly with Prosper and Monette. Mayer and I trusted her and I gave her a briefing on the events. After Brigitte left I reported back to Prosper.

"So what exactly did you tell her?" asked the Colonel.

"Well, the truth, sir."

"The truth?"

"Yes sir, the truth. I told her that the Algerian Muslim population approved of our actions and was completely supportive."

Mayer started to laugh. When the article was published we noticed that it was very much slanted against us. Brigitte wrote Mayer a note to please excuse her: the editors had tampered with her text and she had resigned from the paper. Philippeville was peaceful for the next nine months. Since most petty criminals also happened to be members of the FLN, many had been killed on August 20 and during the days that followed. The town was so quiet and crime-free that the local judge, Voglimacci, took a vacation.

6

Little Messaoud

In the fall, due to the recent events that could bring about reprisals, I decided it would be safer to send my family back to France. Many officers were doing the same thing because the FLN was known to retaliate against the families with any means at their disposal. During a meeting with Superintendent Filiberti, one of his colleagues, Police Superintendent Blanc, had said that to put an end to all this the best thing would be to offer a reward for the top FLN leaders, dead or alive. I thought it was a very good idea and Filiberti agreed with me.

We picked seven names, including Zighoud Youssef and Garsallah Messaoud. We drafted a poster for each man and

Issolah translated it into Arabic to be safe, but it wasn't necessary because among educated Algerian Muslims the majority could read French better than Arabic. The most important parts were the photos of the men we wanted and the amount of money offered as reward. The police superintendent had no funds to make the posters and even less to pay the rewards. We contacted the government's propaganda services, which printed seven versions each of 5,000 flyers and the army air force provided us with a plane.

We picked a few strategic locations to scatter the flyers, the Arab quarter of Philippeville, for the bulk of the leaflets, and the cliff overlooking the air strip for the one concerning Little Messaoud. We also didn't forget the brothel at Philippeville where the madam was a faithful informer for the police commissioner and even went so far, even though she was of the Muslim faith, to close her establishment on Good Friday. After the flyers had been distributed she came running to police headquarters to tell Superintendent Filiberti that the flyers had been very popular with her girls, who had identified several of their regular customers. Little Messaoud's men, once they saw the flyers, began giving their chief some very strange looks, so much so in fact that he began to worry.

In November 1955, the 2nd REP—the paratroop regiment of the Foreign Legion—arrived to replace the 1st RCP that was about to move on to Kenchela, in the Aurès Mountains. My work as intelligence officer in the Philippeville area was therefore to end. However, Colonel Lacapelle, the new area commander, requested that I remain at Philippeville with my entire team and I had to obey without much enthusiasm. He greeted me rather coldly and I quickly transferred my duties to my successors: Captain Happe and Captain Vial.

Happe was an officer specializing in Algerian Muslim affairs and he was appointed as the intelligence officer in the area because he spoke fluent Arabic. Clodius Vial was the intelligence officer of the 2nd REP. Both had a lot of experience but I had to show them the ropes within the region. Beginning in December 1955 we set up a large operation together with the help of Filiberti's men.

We took part in the creation of a regimental commando squad that had brought us a suspect arrested in Philippeville. Issolah and I questioned the man and the interrogation went smoothly, without any violence. The man said he was ready to help us. We had to talk to him calmly for three hours without losing our patience but he seemed to be in good faith and had never done any fighting. He was the gunsmith and in charge of a supply of weapons. He told us about a cave near a burnt forest but was unable despite his honest efforts to pinpoint the spot on the map. Thanks to an observation plane we were able to locate something quite a distance from Philippeville and we decided to set up the operation with that sketchy information.

We marched for a long time and Colonel Masselot, who was in command of the 2nd REP, wanted to turn back. He didn't like me too much and was saying around that I was having a lot success with the ladies, which contributed to his being jealous. Issolah, on the other hand, was with a captain in the Foreign Legion who had a superiority complex.

"Listen here, Sergeant. That information you're touting is really a lot of shit! We've been trudging around for hours for nothing."

"A little more patience, Captain. We must go on, the information is good. I'm sure of it."

To keep the officers from growing even more impatient Issolah had to go up ahead with a squad of Foreign Legion riflemen and they wound up locating the burnt forest. A *fellagha* suddenly appeared and Issolah shot at him with his carbine. The man stopped and immediately tried to get away. Issolah fired again and the *fellagha* lifted only one arm because the NCO had shot him twice in the other arm. The prisoner walked us to the arms cache where we found 150 "stati" Italian rifles,* a few Mausers and some shotguns. Zighoud Youssef was cornered in an ambush by Senegalese troops on the western outskirts of Philippeville, where he was killed with all of his men. The Senegalese infantry was extremely tough. Division headquarters in Constantine told us to improvise for the reward and a commander of the 1st RCP had to give his monthly pay to fulfill the promise.

I was finally able to get a transfer out of Philippeville. And my relations with the new officers in charge were rather tense. Georges Mayer had proposed that I answer a request from army personnel; they were looking for officers to take a course of instruction in England. Candidates had to have experience in air force-related operations, which fit my description and I had been originally trained in Great Britain.

In the spring of 1956 I was sent to a camp at Salisbury for a one-month top-secret training session. There were a

---

* Mannlicher Carcano carbines with a six-cartridge clip. These Italian lightweight rifles were just about everywhere. After the fighting was over in Tunisia in 1943, the rifles littered the battlefields and were used to equip the FLN. [Ed.]

few Frenchmen and some British and Americans being trained in support fire and transport support. We were studying how to embark a paratrooper brigade of 5,000 men for an operation somewhere in the Mediterranean. We had to divide the brigade among various transport planes, pick the airports and estimate the weight. We had prepared a very detailed plan. The loading was assumed to take place in Cyprus and Turkey. We didn't know at the time that we were preparing for the Suez operation. General Gamal Abdel Nasser, the new president of the Republic of Egypt, which had been proclaimed in 1953, wanted the British to leave, which they did at the end of June 1956. One month later he nationalized the Suez Canal. A military action by France and Great Britain, with the participation of Israel, was decided upon at the end of August. The French government knew that Nasser was supporting the FLN. The Suez expedition took place on November 4, 1956 and was successful; however, under pressure from the United States and the USSR, a cease-fire was signed three days later. The operation itself had been prepared since the early spring of that year.

I returned to Algeria in May 1956 and went to Kenchala. Mayer ordered me to remain at the regimental base in Bône and get it reorganized. When I arrived I was told that the high command had decided that the paratroopers would go into training in waves of 1,000 men at a time. It was one more preparation for the Suez expedition. Many regiments had arrived to take part in the jumping exercises. Among them was the 3rd RPC—colonial paratrooper regiment— led by Lieutenant Colonel Marcel Bigeard. I knew him well. We had both been parachuted into the same *maquis* of the Iberian Anarchist Federation in 1944, which was operating in the Ariège region.

Bigeard offered me the opportunity to jump with his unit the next morning, June 1, 1956. I went to see him on the tarmac with his deputy, Lenoir, whom he had nicknamed "my old lady," something Lenoir intensely resented. As a guest I had to jump out first and therefore climb into the plane last. Specialists in Philippeville who worked around the clock folded the parachutes that were then stacked at the field. Each paratrooper would grab one before boarding. I thought I was very lucky to find one once the entire regiment was on board. But luck had nothing to do with it.

The same day at Philippeville, Filiberti had found out that his police station was about to be attacked by FLN commandos. He warned Captain Vial and everyone was ready to give the assailants, none other than Little Messaoud and a dozen men, a big reception. There was an intense hail of gunfire and Little Messaoud and his team were riddled with bullets. Vial was seriously wounded by a 9mm bullet that shattered his hipbone but luckily missed the artery.

In Bône I jumped from an altitude of 400 meters and was very proud to be followed by most of the 3rd RPC. I immediately sensed there was something wrong in the opening of the parachute and felt I could no longer use my right arm. The parachute itself was like a sausage, the hooks were wrapped around the sails and my arm was caught in the harness. I should have immediately opened the lap-pack parachute but I didn't, out of pride toward the 3rd RPC. The ground was coming at me rather fast and I could hear the guys below yelling at me:

"Lap-pack, Lap-pack!"

I thought I had more time, and then at the last minute I grabbed the lap-pack and threw it out in front of me to open it. The lap-pack unfortunately also went up like a candle.

I grabbed it and tried to force it open, then I threw it out again and this time it opened. At that very moment I felt a terrible jolt: I had hit the ground. I didn't feel anything any more. It was beautiful, almost supernatural, seeing all those men coming down from the sky. I could hear some horrible screams from my driver as I attempted and failed to turn toward him. I was paralyzed but had not lost consciousness. Fourteen of us wound up in the hospital.

"You're lucky you only have a spinal fracture," said the nun, who was also the supervisor. "It's better than breaking a leg."

"You must be joking, right sister?"

"Not at all, Captain. The spine mends itself very well, but the legs don't always work the same. I've seen it before."

The surgeon told me he had had the same fracture in a motorcycle accident. I smiled sadly, remembering my crashes in my Harley-Davidson at Fort Montlouis when I was at the headquarters of the 11th Shock battalion.

"Doctor, please tell me the truth. I'll be paralyzed, right?"

"I promise you that I'm going to do everything I can so it won't happen. I'll perform the operation myself and I'll do a good job."

"Should it succeed, will I be able to jump again?"

"In six months."

The doctor was true to his word. He stretched me according to the techniques used by Professor Merle d'Aubigné, a famous surgeon at that time. Then he put me in plaster. I was transferred to the hospital in Algiers and sent back to France. For months while I was completely immobile they dragged me around Paris from one military hospital to the other: first the Percy Hospital in Clamart, then the Villemin near the Gare de l'Est. I returned to Algeria in October 1956.

Much to my chagrin, most of my regiment had left for Cyprus without me. I was forbidden to jump in a parachute until the spring of 1957. But it was still much better than being in a wheelchair.

On November 5, 1956 I was bitter to find out that the 2nd RPC of Philippeville had jumped over Suez the day before. I felt tears welling up in my eyes at the thought of all those men fanning out into the Egyptian sky. My punishment could have been more drastic. I was lucky enough to be assigned temporarily to the regular army and to be involved in a war where paratroopers were being used for the first time to their full capacity. I had become an invalid. I was bitter because I had prepared that operation down to its smallest detail! The 1st REP had landed but my regiment had been left behind on Cyprus. That was my only consolation.

7

Algiers

I returned to Chebli in the Mitidja, where the rear base of my regiment was under the command of Major Lafargue, a happy old comrade-in-arms whose nickname was "Pétanque."* He was a few years older than me and we had gone through the Saint-Maixent officer's school together. I was staying at a villa that Robert Martel had provided to Colonel Mayer.

Martel was a *pied-noir*, a determined supporter of *Algérie Française*, and a well-respected and very influential local poli-

---

* Pétanque is the French word for the game of bocce. [Ed.]

tician. He had also lent us several farms to serve as barracks
for our other units. Chebli was very quiet and I didn't know
anyone in town. Lafargue had very good relations with the
sector next to ours, which was being patrolled by the 3rd
RCA (Régiment de Cavalerie Africaine), an armored unit
under the command of Major Antoine Argoud. At least they
were seeing a lot of action. The cavalry of the 3rd RCA was
fighting very hard on the mountain close by, a part of the
Blida-Atlas chain. We were unable to go and help out because we were only about 100 men just transferred in or
recovering from various war wounds.

I had just been promoted to Major and could no longer
be an intelligence officer because from now on I was the
regimental commander working with the Colonel on the
ordinary administration of the unit. Lafargue was envious
of my job and kept repeating that even if I worked hard I
could probably get everything done in a single hour per day.
But sinecures were not for me and I was getting bored very
quickly, so I began taking stock of events very carefully.

The situation had become much worse during my ab-
sence. Several dozen attacks were taking place every day,
especially in Algiers where the FLN had decided to broaden
its scope. The majority of the city's population was *pied-noir*
and the FLN was hoping to scare them into fleeing Algeria.
The "autonomous zone," or ZAA (*Zone Autonome d'Alger*),
which was both a political and military organization, had
been set up by the FLN to patrol the Muslim areas of Algiers,
and the Casbah in particular, an old town made up of a
series of narrow streets laid out as a maze, where houses all
had inner courtyards and terraces offering the rebels ideal
places to hide and operate. The objective of this "autonomous zone" was to greatly increase the number of terrorist

incidents and quickly force the government into a dead-end. There were at the time three to four daily attacks inside Algiers, mainly targeting civilians and the tendency was clearly on the increase.

The Algiers "autonomous zone" and its suburban area was under the control of a 33-year-old man named Larbi Ben M'Hidi, who came from a family of well-to-do farmers and had studied the theater before getting involved in subversive activities. His idea was to accelerate terrorism to such a crescendo that France would be compelled to abandon Algeria and he expected an increasingly tough reaction from French authorities because his attacks were becoming more and more spectacular. On September 30, bombs had exploded at the Milk Bar and the Cafeteria—popular hangouts for young French people in Algiers. There were four people killed and fifty-two wounded, often losing their limbs. Ben M'Hidi had very able deputies in Yacef Saadi, a 28-year-old baker in the Casbah, and the very dangerous Ali-la-Pointe. At that time I still didn't know that I was destined to play a role in the lives of those men and didn't even know their names.

During the month of November 1956, terror was everywhere around Algiers. On the afternoon of November 13 three bombs were thrown by FLN agents, one into a bus at the Hussein-Dey bus station, with thirty-six casualties; another in a department store with nine persons seriously injured; and the third in a railroad station. The next day, Fernand Yveton, an employee of the gas and electric company of Algeria, who also happened to be an active member of the PCA, was arrested just as he had placed a time bomb in his locker inside the gas plant. Another worker had overheard the ticking of the bomb's timer, and had warned the authorities. Some very fast police work established that Yveton had prepared a second bomb. Fortunately the timer and detonator had malfunctioned and the bomb was discovered intact a few hours later behind central police headquarters.

On November 28, three bombs exploded in downtown Algiers. They had been placed on the same day and at the same time, which required a very large organization. From the head of the "autonomous zone" down to the foot soldiers actually placing the bombs required a complex structure with many accomplices on the ground—informers, purveyors of explosives, specialists in firing techniques, people providing accommodations, etc.—that meant thousands of volunteers. Just before Christmas, one month later, a bomb in a school bus killed and maimed several children. Yet the assassinations of Aït Ali, who was president of the administrative council of Algiers, and even more that of Amédée Froger, mayor of Boufarik and president of the Mayors Federation of Algeria, by Ali Amar, also known as Ali-la-Pointe, made a bigger impression on the public. On December 30, during Froger's burial service, a demonstration of about 20,000 persons took to the streets of Algiers and some of them vented their anger by lynching Muslims at random.

My regiment returned from Cyprus at the end of December 1956 in this atmosphere charged with fear. My former deputies were back, except for Issolah, who had been sent to officer's school, and Soutiras. As replacements we got a schoolteacher named Zamid, who was a draftee from Tunisia and Babaye, a former *fellagha*. These men now reported to Captain Assémat, the new intelligence officer who had replaced me. The captain was having a hard time in gaining acceptance because the men resented the fact that he had remained as a cavalry school instructor in Morocco rather that going to Indochina and getting himself killed just like everyone else.

I stayed on at Chebli until the beginning of 1957. I was hoping to see the regiment go back into action but there were no immediate plans for that. The FLN apparently feared reactions from the French army in the wake of the Suez operation. We all felt very disappointed because that operation, which had started so well, had to be aborted for political and diplomatic reasons. We were eagerly seeking revenge.

On January 7, 1957 Prosper got a phone call from Colonel Godard, who was the second-in-command of the 10th Paratrooper Division.

"Massu has just been appointed to an exceptionally important position. He is becoming the Super-Prefect of the city of Algiers and the northern part of the department. He's moving into the Prefecture and needs to create a new staff. Send us two of your officers."

"For what kind of job?"

"The job isn't definite right now, but it has to do with maintaining law and order and protecting the population from FLN terrorism."

The minister-in-residence, Robert Lacoste, had delegated his police powers to Massu and his 10th DP with the mission of "eliminating terrorism from the greater city of Algiers." Mayer called me in to relate his conversation with Godard, asking me which names I would propose. After the months I had spent at Philippeville and seeing how things were shaping up in Algiers I had no trouble imagining the kind of mission the government had given to Massu. Since it was impossible to get rid of urban terrorism through normal police and judicial procedure, they were asking the paratroopers to replace both the policemen and the judges. Should they object that it was not a job for soldiers, the answer was that the rebels had decided to wage war inside the city through terror and the army was simply fulfilling its mission by taking them on. The urban terrorist and the *fellagha* in the mountains were one and the same enemy. I understood the logic of the argument but for no money in the world did I want to get involved in such a mission, because clearly we were about to get our hands dirty.

To name two officers to be on Massu's staff was not handing them a gift: it was sending them after 5,000 terrorists who were mixed in with the rest of the population, with all the risks of failure that could amount to. The interested parties could only look forward to being disowned by their own leadership and promised general opprobrium.

"I don't think I need to think too long. I have both names," I answered with a smile.

I knew of two lieutenants with almost the same sounding last names who could fit the bill: Charbonnier and Arbonnier. A few months before both had asked to leave the regiment and because of that they were not too well liked. Charbonnier was a former reserve officer-candidate and thought promotions and advancement were too slow at the 1st RCP. He had tried to join the ALAT but failed and had been returned to us. Because of his request he had become very unpopular with his commanding officers, Captain Bizard and Major Masselot, nicknamed Botéla. Transferring him to a police job was a very dirty trick because nothing could be farther from what he was hoping for.

Arbonnier was a former NCO who had been sent to the 4th Company and would be very happy to leave because he was requesting to do so anyway. Both lieutenants didn't know what they were getting into and were happy to be leaving the regiment.

Godard called back a few hours later. The situation had changed. Massu wanted not just two staff officers but also a commanding officer to be his deputy within a parallel staff he was setting up at the same time. The problem was that I was designated to be the commanding officer.

"Massu wants you to join his group," said Mayer, somewhat subdued. "Godard just called me about it."

"But why me, goddamn shit?"

"It's because of Philippeville. Massu was very impressed by the work you did over there."

"You shouldn't have told him anything. You put me in the shit. Godard is getting out of it and playing a dirty trick on me."

"Even if I kept silent Massu would have found out about Philippeville anyway. And stop yelling at me about it! The orders could also be coming from higher up and the mission may not be so bad after all."

"Not so bad? You must be joking? You know what they'll ask me to do? They'll have me do the dirty work, all of it! It's going to be Philippeville all right, but ten times worse. I wasn't born to clean out the Casbah!"

"Are you under some strange notion that we're not all going to be drafted into this? Godard and the staff are wiggling out of it, but do you think they won't send the regiments of the 10th DP to the meat grinder?"

"I don't give a damn anyway. I won't go! I refuse!"

"So what will we do?"

"Why not send Pétanque! He looks like Massu, two loud mouths who are made for each other. Tell Massu and Godard whatever you want but I'm going to stay right here."

Mayer got very concerned seeing me all worked up like that. He called in Lafargue, who agreed to take my place and then phoned Massu to try and get him to accept. But the General lost his patience and was not the type of person to be thwarted for very long nor hoodwinked by one of his staff.

"Listen, Mayer, that's enough! You send me Aussaresses on the double! Understood?"

"And if he doesn't want to, General?"

"I couldn't care less if he doesn't want to. He'll come just the same."

Beyond the staff at the Prefecture that was being put together by taking two officers from every regiment of the 10th DP, or about ten in all, Massu thought it necessary to set up a "parallel" staff, which was actually a code word for "secret." That team was to include two deputies of unimpeachable loyalty. The first officer had already been picked. He happened to be an old acquaintance of mine, Lieutenant Colonel Roger Trinquier, who also came from special services. Trinquier was Massu's comrade-in-arms and his closest confidant. His task was to draft a counter-subversion plan that included a population control mechanism.

Trinquier and Massu were very close, having each been named Second-Lieutenant on the same day, one from Saint-Cyr and the other from Saint-Maixent. Trinquier originally came from the Basses-Alpes and would have become a schoolteacher had he not discovered his military calling when he was drafted and trained as an intelligence officer. He was a smart soldier with a lot of curiosity and imagination in all his initiatives. After a tough time in a colonial unit, he had been part of the French garrison in Shanghai. He was very much taken with Asia. At the end of the war he saw action in Indochina in one of the first battalions of colonial paratroopers and then had been in command of the GCMA, or mixed airborne combat group. It was a special forces unit connected to the SDECE with a mission to operate behind Viet Minh lines and gather information necessary for airborne operations.

Trinquier was the type of person who could easily adapt to any situation and could succeed at the most difficult missions. He had been appointed commander of the airborne center of French North Africa in Algeria, an independent unit located at Blida Air Base, with instructional and operational missions. That base was the supervisory unit for the parachute jumping schools. I knew Trinquier quite well, having met him in Indochina and once my battalion was disbanded I was one of the first to be transferred to the GCMA.

Massu needed two deputies, Trinquier for intelligence gathering and a second officer for action implementation. The second deputy was to be in constant contact with the police departments, regimental commanders and their intelligence officers. Massu had picked me for that job, which amounted to a smart choice since I knew so many people in the field by now. Unless the order emanated from higher up the idea had almost certainly come from Godard, and not out of good feelings. Godard didn't want to appear to be taking on the role of the prefects and their administration that Massu had been assigned to take over. He also openly disapproved of using the division as a police force within Algiers and wanted the 10th DP to remain ready for any and all outside assignments, which was part of its original mission. It also meant keeping the divisional staff headquarters unchanged and located at Hydra, in the western suburb of Algiers. All this meant that Massu would be operating on his own.

Godard and I knew each other well and didn't like each other at all since he took over my duties in 1948 as commander of the 11th Shock battalion, a unit I had set up single-handedly. I can safely state that he even pulled some strings to take my job and his taking over the unit had gone very badly. Godard wanted me to stay as his deputy and promised me a very quick promotion, but you can't play second fiddle once you've led the entire band. That was just about the way I answered him. When I got to Montlouis in 1946 I gathered 35 veterans of the assault troops of the Free French Forces, who all looked like weirdos then. Two years later I handed over to Godard an elite unit of some 850 dedicated commandos.

Godard's style, more like a caricature of the professional soldier, was far removed from mine. Four officers of section 29—Bichelot, Chaunien, Pioche, and Maloubier—who had been on temporary assignment to the battalion and deeply regretted the kind of special spirit I had instilled into "Bagheera"—the nickname we had given to the unit—sported a subtle mix of anarchy and discipline, artistic freedom and ascetic living. They walked out as soon as the new commander arrived. Godard couldn't understand, for instance, the kind of personal statement by a soldier who had formerly been part of His Majesty's special services, consisting of adopting the British stance at attention, with clenched fists. Nor could he accept that another commando should arrive in the courtyard of Vauban's citadel piloting his Harley-Davidson like a daredevil, wearing a Laotian sarong, with a pretty girl on the rear seat. I was known to accept that kind of craziness, and it is possible that I even encouraged it. Which was why I was always thought of as an oddball. The more narrow-minded types said I was nothing but an intellectual, i.e., a faggot, a communist and an antimilitarist.

I couldn't refuse Massu. Either I took his offer or I had to resign my commission. To leave the army meant leaving the special services and betraying my ideals. So I climbed into my jeep and reluctantly drove off toward Algiers.

8

The Mission

Trinquier and I were therefore appointed almost at the same time. Massu had picked us for our unimpeachable military spirit and our uncompromising dedication to discipline, which could appear a contradiction in terms since we were both staunch non-conformists and displayed a lot of independent thinking. Massu however, knew we wouldn't betray him. That was of paramount importance and he was right. Furthermore, Trinquier and I always got along very well.

I reported to Massu on January 8, 1957 with a sinking feeling. I was really wondering what was happening to me.

My military career was dead in the water anyway and that was a fact I had to accept. Massu was 50. He was impressive because of his height and extraordinary personality. He was a great soldier and knowing it he took many liberties. He had been stationed in Morocco after graduating from Saint-Cyr, taking part in the Rif War and the fighting at Djebel Sarho. After that he participated in the Campaign of France with the Leclerc division. In Indochina he recaptured Hanoi in 1946 with such energy that Emperor Bao Daï requested his transfer back to France. Massu had mopped up the city using mortar fire and taking no prisoners.

Massu was full of energy and made absolutely no allowances. Once he took command of the 10th DP we could expect him to use tough methods if necessary. We were to have good, but never close, relations. We could have become friends had I told him that his wife had seen me when I was still a small child. My father, who had been a deputy-prefect and a sergeant during the First World War, had a soldier in his unit by the name of Henry Torrès, who wanted to beat up the lieutenant. The sergeant was able to talk Torrès out of it amicably. Shortly after that incident Torrès' father died and François Aussaresses had granted him leave and even gave him some cash to travel to the funeral. The sergeant and the soldier met again in Paris. My father had become the chief of staff to the minister of the PTT and Torrès was now one of the leading attorneys in the French capital. They would meet often and one day Torrès brought his wife-to-be, Suzanne Rosambert, to our house. With the outbreak of war Suzanne and Henri Torrès, who were both Jewish, had to leave for the United States. Mrs. Torrès quickly enlisted in the Free French Forces and became a major. She was in charge of the women in the

Leclerc division that were called the "Rochambelles" and her nickname was Toto. She met Massu in Saigon after her divorce, so now she was my boss' wife. Since I had nothing to lose, I didn't mince my words when I was in front of Massu:

"General, I'd rather tell you straight away that I didn't volunteer for this assignment. I didn't volunteer at all!"

"I know old man," he answered with a sly smile. "It only proves that you have understood what is expected of you and that's all for the better. We're going to make up for lost time on the double. Be aware that you are the man of the hour. That's why you were picked. As we speak the FLN rules Algiers and is reminding us of that fact every day. It's also letting the entire world know. Not only is the FLN running amok in the city, its main leadership is also located there and everyone knows it. Today, Aussaresses, we are going to knock them off very quickly and by every possible means. These are the government's orders. Since you weren't volunteering for the job you're well aware that this is not an assignment for the choirboys."

Massu took me in his Peugeot 403, driving at top speed through Algiers. It was a beautiful and very lively city with a population of over one million, including the suburban areas. The demographics were the reverse of the rest of Algeria, since the Algerian Muslim population was in the minority among a majority of *pieds-noirs*. Once we reached the Prefecture, the General showed me my office, which was next to his. To create an administrative cover for me he had an announcement typed up that stated in very terse language that Major Aussaresses was in charge of relations between General Massu, the police, and district attorney, which in plain language meant that I had to have such good relations with the policemen that I could use them and be sure we would never need to contact the judiciary.

Then Massu took me aside and whispered:

"Aussaresses, I must tell you something no one else knows besides you and me. I have just had a meeting with the most important *pieds-noirs* in society, both in Algeria and the city of Algiers. These people are very determined. They told me they intend to replace the police and military forces if these are still incapable of resolving the situation. They intend to begin with a spectacular event because they're convinced that the geographic nerve center of the FLN is located inside the Casbah. They are not wrong in that assumption. The Casbah is on an incline and at the top there is a wide avenue. They want to bring a truck convoy filled with gasoline, have the first truck stop and tighten the line of the other trucks, bumper to bumper, and then they'll open the gaskets. Once the gasoline has washed deep into the Casbah they'll set it on fire. According to my estimate about 70,000 people will die. Believe me when I tell you that the men I was speaking with can make this happen. The determination of these *pieds-noirs* compels me to take a very tough attitude. They're not fooling around. It's going to be very hard, Aussaresses, and we'll have to be implacable."

"Implacable" meant using torture and summary executions. I bowed and felt defeated.

"I understand, General."

"We are under the threat of a strike that will turn into an insurrection set for Monday, January 28."

"What's the significance of that date?" I asked.

"Because on the same day there's a UN general assembly. An FLN delegation will be present to attempt to start a debate on the Algerian issue. France will naturally say that the UN is not a competent forum; however, the strike is a way to show that the FLN does represent the Algerian people."

"What should I do?"

"Break the strike. You've got less than 20 days."

"And how do you expect me to do it?"

"Make arrests and question all the organizers."

"But how will I know who to arrest? It takes months to set up an intelligence network."

"Use the police files."

"Which branch?"

"You'll have to find that out for yourself. All I can tell you is that the police have a secret file that will be very useful to your mission."

"And you're convinced that the police will agree to let me have the file?"

"Figure that out for yourself; it's your job now."

By discussing the possibility of a new Saint Bartholomew's Massacre by the *pieds-noirs*, Massu had removed my last hesitation and I decided to help him as best I could, come what may. I was about to leave his office when he called me back:

"Oh yes, I almost forgot. There's an underground anti-military newspaper called *La Voix du soldat*. Paris wants very much to find out who's supporting this enterprise and also would appreciate it if that rag would disappear. Permanently. Understood?"

"Understood, General."

He hadn't said anything about the length of the mission; my transfer was a temporary assignment that was to last no more than six months. I was convinced everything would be wrapped up long before that. It would last a couple of weeks at the most.

The web I had created in Philippeville was useless to me in this large city. My only contact with the police force was Superintendent Arnassan, former head of the Renseigments Généraux in Philippeville, who had just been transferred to Algiers. He would be able to recommend me to his colleagues. I quickly made a list of whoever was in a position to help me outside the police force, the head of military security and the representative of the special services. I was still in contact with the reserve officers of the service and we had helped each other out more than once. I had even met with Jacques Morlanne in Algiers, together with Colonel Germain, one of the agents Morlanne had set up there. Germain was officially a history professor and had been transferred to Algiers by the SDECE in June 1955. He was in charge of organizing a mission out of Algiers to eliminate the FLN leaders outside Algerian territory. In the course of that mission Germain had succeeded with the government's approval, in engineering the arrest of Ahmed Ben Bella, whose DC3, while en route from Ra-bat, Morocco, was forced into landing in Algiers on October 22, 1956. Germain was disowned by the government because of that mission and subsequently went back to teaching.

The men of the "dairy" were swarming in Algiers by now, ever since General Lorillot had complained that he couldn't understand why there was no involvement of the special services in Algeria. The 11th Shock battalion had been sent in under the command of Colonel Decorse, whom I knew, since we had worked together in Indochina. Most of the officers of that group had been trained at the center for special mission leaders that I had headed. But the 11th

Shock only took part in specific missions, either to manufacture booby-trapped attaché cases meant for the *fellagha* or to recruit members of the MNA party, the rival nationalist movement founded by Messali Hadj, that the FLN had vowed to liquidate down to the last man.

Jacques Morlanne had also tried to set up a Mediterranean Action Service based in Tangier and handled by the gangster Jo Attia, a former lieutenant of Pierrot le Fou in the "traction" automobile gang. But Jo Attia, who had Bob Maloubier as his case officer hadn't been very convincing. The few missions he had been given, mostly inside Morocco, had failed and the whole thing ended in a huge fiasco. Later on Jo Attia lost his head and tried to return to France despite the fact that he had been deported. When he was brought before the judge he asked the magistrate to dial NOR 00 90, which was the switchboard number of the SDECE, and ask to speak with Mr. Lefort—his real name was Didier Faure-Beaulieu. The matter reached the minister of justice, who demanded an explanation from Bour-sicaud, the director general of the SDECE, during a cabinet meeting. Boursicaud was of a mind to dissolve the Action Service but in the end he only decided to fire Morlanne, who was replaced by Colonel Rousillat. They also suggested to Bob Maloubier that he go and nurse his old war wounds in Switzerland and forget the SDECE.

In any case, even though I was not actually aware of it, I had become the Special Services man inside the battle of Algiers.

9

The *Préfecture*

Massu assigned me a clever and congenial lieutenant named Gérard Garcet as my deputy. He had been Massu's ADC until then but had fallen from grace due to an incident involving some rotten shrimp he had forgotten in a refrigerator. A few days before, Massu, having just returned from Egypt, wanted to relax and go fishing. He had sent his ADC to find some shrimp to be used as bait. While Garcet was off on his errand, General Raoul Salan had summoned Massu, informing him of his new mission and sending him off to see the resident minister, Robert Lacoste. Once the lieutenant, who had lots of trouble finding the bait and was looking forward to going fishing, returned, he found the house empty. The General having disappeared, Garcet concluded that the fishing expedition had been cancelled without his being informed. Garcet was disappointed and got rid of the bait by hiding it inside the refrigerator. Day after day the Massu family meals had taken on an increasingly strange taste and apparently Jacques Massu was much more sensitive than his wife to taste and smell.

"But Suzanne, don't you think the meat has a strange taste, and the vegetables too?"

"Jacques, you're really being very difficult. Maybe you think someone wants to poison you?"

The General could take no more and running to the kitchen he followed the smell to the refrigerator and discovered what his ADC had done. Garcet had been violently reprimanded and sought revenge by stealing a case of Scotch whiskey that his "ingrate" of a boss had brought back from Egypt. The whiskey found its way to our office and helped us get through the many tough nights ahead.

I had to start my new job by making the rounds of visits according to protocol. Some of them had to take place with Massu. We started with the prefect of the Algiers region, Serge Baret, who was very friendly and cooperative. Then we met with Paul Teitgen, the general secretary of the Prefecture, who had been in charge of the Algiers police for four months. Massu and every paratrooper knew Teitgen as the man who had driven General Faure out of Algeria. General Faure was to eventually return; however, in January 1960, after the barricades by the French ultras in Algiers, he was suspected of having "Algérie Française" sympathies and was again ordered back to France.

Faure was a patriotic Frenchman but during the Second World War he had refused to join General de Gaulle and had even traveled to London to tell him as much. Vichy noticed that this very non-conformist officer was steadfastly anti-German and decided to ship him out to Morocco, where he was put in charge of the youth service. Following the allied landings in November 1942 he had taken part in the creation of the 1st RCP, culled from airborne infantry units. There was even a legend going around that de Gaulle's personal hatred of General Faure eventually affected the 1st RCP to the point that the regiment was never allowed to take part in a single paratrooper operation. In Algeria Faure had been in command of mountain troops.

General Faure felt that French military policy towards the rebels in Algeria wasn't vigorous enough and he didn't hold back his views. Paul Teitgen had been kept informed of the General's attitude and had decided to record his statements. When Faure came to visit, Teitgen encouraged him to speak up once he activated the tape recorder. The tapes were almost inaudible but Teitgen was able to transcribe them and sent them on to Paris with a request to have General Faure recalled to France, placed under arrest, and relieved of his command because of his involvement in a "plot." Teitgen succeeded and the incident made the rounds of every barracks in Algeria. Every military man in the area now despised the general secretary because they resented underhanded police methods being used against a superior officer.

Massu and I were sitting in Teitgen's office waiting for him to appear. Massu showed me the furniture that had been used to hide the tape recorder and whispered maliciously to me:

"What you're looking at is the desk with the tape recorder. So be careful about what you say in here!"

The conversation we had with the general secretary was polite and very formal. Teitgen never hinted that he knew about the true nature of my mission. We agreed on the procedures to be used when making arrests. It was obvious to everyone that the justice system would be swamped with cases. The Prefecture was to take special administrative measures towards those we brought in for questioning. They were to be placed under house arrest using a departmental order issued by the Prefecture that Teitgen would sign and that would legitimize our initiatives. The prison system was going to be too small since we expected many arrests. We decided to use a "triage" camp in an old school building in the Algiers suburb called Beni-Messous. Those under house arrest were to be sorted out and routed to other camps to the south; the best known being in the village called Paul-Cazelles, later renamed Aïn Oussera once Algeria became independent.

Teitgen appointed Charles Ceccaldi-Reynaud, a former attorney who had become a police superintendent, as administrator of the Beni-Messous camp, with Police Inspector Devichi as his deputy. Ceccaldi-Reynaud has since become the mayor of Puteaux, a town on the outskirts of Paris, and a Member of Parliament. Massu didn't trust Teitgen and decided to place the camp under guard by a military unit, assigning a battalion of engineer draftees for the task. The General then took me to a meeting, which included regimental commanders and area commanders such as General de Bollardière and Colonel Argoud. Massu gave his men a long pep talk.

"Gentlemen, your mission is to take back the night from the FLN in Algiers. First, you will set up a curfew and shall give orders to fire at will on anyone who doesn't respect it. I am counting on you to be operational on a 24-hour basis."

Argoud got up and said to Massu:

"No, General, only 23 hours and 45 minutes. I'm just asking for 15 minutes to sleep."

The officers roared with laughter.

I never saw Bollardière present at those meetings after that, since he decided to place some distance between himself and the methods used by the 10th DP in Algiers and was to make statements to the press against the use of torture. In March 1957 he asked to be transferred to another assignment. Besides his personal complaints, Bollardière couldn't accept the fact that Massu had been critical of his meager results in the struggle against the FLN. I am not certain that the issue of torture was the sole reason for Bollardière's hostility toward Massu. I knew "Bolo" quite well because I had been his deputy in Indochina in 1951 in the colonial brigade in Cochinchine. It was rumored that there had been personal animosity between him and Massu going back to the taking of Hanoi in 1946.

On the same day I visited Superintendent Arnassan, who confirmed that there indeed was a mysterious card file that General Massu had mentioned to me. It contained some 2,000 names of FLN leaders in Algiers and the greater region around the city. The files had been set up by the RG whichever way they could and this prevented it from being used by other services. Arnassan let me use the files so that I could have them copied by the officers working at Prefecture headquarters. This was a necessary tool to get our work started and as new arrests were being made and more people were questioned the files grew proportionately. Arnassan also introduced me to all his colleagues and to Superintendent Parat, who was in charge of the criminal police force.

I began making the rounds and meeting people with the same determination as when I arrived at Philippeville two years before. Many of the people I was meeting would inquire as to Massu's real importance in the scheme of things. Massu had an ambiguous position as a General and Super-Prefect because most of his tasks, which were out of the ordinary, had an aura of mystery about them.

"At which level do you place your General, exactly?"

"At the highest level."

"Of course, but who would he be reporting to directly?"

"To the government."

"The general government of Algeria?"

"No, to the government of the French Republic."

This was absolutely true and therefore the police function that Massu had delegated to me was particularly important. On January 30, 1956 socialist Guy Mollet became prime minister, replacing Edgar Faure. François Mitterrand was appointed minister of justice and Maurice Bourgès-Maunoury, the former minister of the interior under Edgar Faure, was now minister of defense, with Max Lejeune as his state secretary. General Catroux, who favored giving independence to the colonies, had been named minister resident in Algeria the day before the Mollet government was formed. But General Catroux was in favor of decolonizing and he decided to resign on February 6, 1956. Guy Mollet replaced him with Robert Lacoste, a socialist party politician, who favored taking a tough stance against the FLN.

Many *pied-noir* political leaders called on me. They were very impressed by the "highest level" we were now working from and they knew that my regimental headquarters at Chebli was in one of Robert Martel's farmhouses and Martel happened to be one of the most influential among the *pied-noir* leaders. He also came to see me and helped me on many occasions. But I didn't just get acquainted with the Algiers "establishment." I repeated what I had done in Philippeville and met with shopkeepers and especially those who ran bistros. I admit that this wasn't the worse part of my mission but it was extremely useful to me. I often met with Pietri, who ran a bistro called *L'Ile-de-Beauté*, located right in front of the Prefecture. The barber next door to the bistro was also a very big help, as well as Guillaume the Italian, who was a former Foreign Legionnaire and always wore a green necktie and reigned supreme at the *Cintra*, the elegant bar at the Aletti Hotel.

The curfew that Massu had ordered was quickly established. The patrols followed orders and started shooting at anything that moved. They left the dead in the streets where they had been shot: there was no time to take care of the bodies and the population had to see them. To acquire credibility the paratroopers had to be even more extreme than the FLN. This kind of summary execution in the streets of Algiers would prove that the government was fully determined to prevail and that we were its enforcers. The effect was such that the very next day denunciations began coming in. All four regiments were active during the first nights of the curfew. On the night of January 15-16, 1957, for instance, they combed the Casbah and several thousand suspects were questioned. During the day patrols and sentries were guarding the critical points of the city.

One such operation that took place in the center of Algiers very close to military headquarters made the news in early 1957. A soldier who was patrolling a street corner saw an Algerian Muslim enter a building to throw a hand grenade. The soldier waited outside for the man to come out and shot him. The terrorist was killed. The dean of the Algiers law school, Jacques Peyrega, was in the same street at the time and saw the soldier shoot the man. Had he witnessed the entire incident or only the conclusion? In any case Peyrega wrote a letter to the minister of national defense, Bourgès-Maunoury, protesting what he thought was a summary execution. He sent a copy of the letter to the newspaper *Le Monde*, which published it on April 5. Upon reading the paper a delegation of law school students came to the Prefecture to show their solidarity with Massu and denounce the position taken by the *"fellagha* dean." My deputy, Garcet, spoke with the students, who were determined to take action. They wanted to teach Peyrega a lesson and Garcet, seeing that they were not joking and fearing that the whole thing could turn into a public lynching, found a way to quiet them down. Garcet promised to use half a dozen young officers dressed in civilian clothes and teach the dean a lesson. They would attend classes using forged student ID cards. The students liked the idea so much that they volunteered to forge the ID cards, allowing access to the university buildings. I had to support Garcet's initiative. However, the dean had received threatening letters after his letter was published and returned to France on April 9, 1957; so the punishment, which had been planned in great detail, was never meted out.

When the 1st RCP entered Algiers, my accommodations were a very modest private house. Colonel Mayer and his wife were living in a spacious house in the more expensive section of Algiers, near the Sesini Villa, which was the headquarters of the 1st REP. Captain Faulques was the regimental intelligence officer and one of the very few to come back alive from the disaster at Cao Bang in Indochina, where he had almost been cut in half by machine gun fire. He had been evacuated, thanks to an emergency landing strip I had built in the area.

Since Faulques and I were living alone the Mayers offered to have us share their house. To have three men and one woman living under the same roof led to gossip. One captain of the 1st REP, who was obviously taken by Monette Mayer, made a ridiculous and unwarranted scene in my presence one day when I actually spent very little time at the Mayer house. I only went there during the day to get some sleep. Garcet and I had to get our logistics organized and I paid a visit to Colonel Godard to get a car assigned. He was very quick to answer that I should ask my regiment for one. So a jeep and a driver were provided by the 1st RCP. Later on my lieutenant was able to get a luxury sedan that we "inherited" from a wealthy *fellagha*.

It was urgent that we form a team to help us operate. Garcet identified about 20 experienced NCOs from various regiments, including mine, that were assigned to divisional headquarters while they were waiting to be transferred to other non-paratrooper units. Since they were inactive I asked Massu to let me have them, to which he agreed, on condition that the men agree to serve in my unit. I called in the men and told them that if they agreed to be on my team they would have to take brutal action and could expect very little from this temporary assignment, at the conclusion of which they would, in any case, have to leave the paratroopers. They all agreed. Two among the men owed me: Chief Warrant Officer Barrat and Sergeant Major

Fontaine, who had both been involved in fistfights with civilians in Philippeville. I had taken steps with Mayer to make sure they were not prosecuted. There was also André Orsoni, an extremely discreet man who had been awarded the Legion of Honor, which was something very rare for an NCO, for unusual bravery. I also remember Averinos, a Legionnaire of Greek national origin.

Babaye, the former *fellagha*, who was a huge hulk of a black man from the region south of Constantine, was also part of the group. My Philippeville unit had captured him in the Aurès Mountains during my convalescence after my accident. Babaye was taking cover behind some rocks, fighting off the paratroopers like a lion, but he was too far away for them to throw a hand grenade. Once he finished his ammunition he came out with his hands above his head and surrendered.

"But he's a 'babaye'"—a black man in the local dialect. "What's he doing here?"

When they questioned him my men found that they liked the guy. He came from the region around Biskra, where many Africans were employed as masseurs in the public baths and basically treated like slaves.

"Why did you join the *fellagha*?"

"They didn't ask for my approval."

"Why not join us?"

"Why not? I don't give a damn."

Babaye worked with me throughout the battle of Algiers.

I used some penetration agents. One of them had infiltrated the FLN leadership and became the agent handling Yacef Saadi. Thanks to him we were able to arrest Yacef Saadi long after I left Algeria, which led to the death of Ali-la-Pointe and the end of the battle of Algiers. On some nights I would slip away without telling anyone and Garcet took charge of the team. None of the men knew I had a second team that included Pierre Misiry, Maurice Jacquet, Yves Cuomo, and Zamid, the schoolteacher. I used two completely separate groups that knew nothing about each another: it was a safety net should someone in authority seek to find out what we were doing during our strange nightly runs.

10

2000 Leopards

At first, Massu was basically improvising as he went about setting up the new structure; soon it became well organized. Full use of Arnassan's files allowed me to draw up lists of suspects and to proceed with massive arrests. Interrogations of suspects led us to new names and with my files growing through sources mainly provided by Colonel Roger Trinquier, whose personal passion for the history of Napoleon's saga was to be extremely helpful in his new mission. He noticed that when Napoleon proceeded to administer the cities he had just captured in the Rhine valley, he began by numbering each house and counting and identifying its inhabitants. Trinquier used the same method in Algiers.

Policemen, gendarmes, CRS, and even soldiers were used to carry out this task under the guise of the *Détachement de protection urbaine* (DPU). Under the supervision of the officers on the Prefecture's staff lists of names were established. They would ask the oldest dweller of a house to name each person who was living there. That information was crosschecked with statements made by the neighbors so that those who were absent thus became suspects. When they returned they were automatically questioned. The results of the interrogations and comparisons of various sources allowed the patrols to set up reliable lists of persons we should be looking for.

Algiers and its greater area were divided into four zones, each one under the control of one paratrooper infantry regiment: the 1st RCP, the 1st REP, and the 2nd and 3rd RPCs. My regiment, the 1st RCP under Georges Mayer's command, was located at Maison-Carrée. His intelligence officer was Captain Assémat, who had taken over my job. The 1st REP was under the leadership of Albert Brothier— the brother-in-law of André Guelfi, nicknamed Dédé la Sardine because of the fishing company he owned in Morocco—the regimental deputy commander was Lieutenant Colonel Jeanpierre, who very quickly took over overall command. During World War II Jeanpierre had been sent to a concentration camp by the Nazis. I met him in Indochina where he was the deputy commander of the 1st battalion of Foreign Legion paratroopers. We fought in the same battle for the *Route Coloniale* number 4. Jeanpierre was killed after the battle of Algiers, during an attack north of Constantine. Captain Faulques was the intelligence officer

headquartered at the Villa Sésini. The 1st REP was originally known as the 1st Battalion of Foreign Legion Paratroopers, created in 1948 and wiped out during the retreat
from Cao Bang, near Vietnam's border with China, in October 1950.

Colonel Albert Fossey-François, who was to lose his life
after the Algerian war during a parachute jump, led the
2nd RPC. He was a colorful and warm-hearted man, a
former literature student who had working in publishing
and printing before joining the special services during
World War II. He was the commander of one of the three
battalions in my regiment in Indochina. In Algiers his intelligence officer was Lieutenant Deiber. Fossey-François
had come to replace Lieutenant Colonel Château-Jobert,
also known as Conan, who was in command of the 2nd
RPC during the Suez operation. Château-Jobert had been
trained in England and parachuted into occupied France and
Holland. In Indochina he had been second in command to
de Bollardière.

The 3rd RPC was led by Lieutenant Colonel Marcel
Bigeard, with Captain Jacques Allaire as his intelligence officer; both men had fought gallantly at the battle of Dien
Bien Phu. Lieutenant Colonel Perrin, one of my fellow officers at the *Action Service*, was the commanding officer of a
regiment of airborne artillery that along with a unit of engineers made up the entire division's forces. The area of Alger-
Sahel had a traditional military structure under the leadership of Colonel Jean Marey. The 9th Zouaves of Colonel
Bargeot, with Captain Sirvent as intelligence officer, was
essentially active inside the Casbah and helped us immea-
surably during our mission.

We agreed with Police Superintendent Parat that a police detective would be working alongside each intelligence officer. This worked out very well because I made sure that the policemen and the officers would get along. The policemen were wearing leopard camouflage uniforms when they went out with the units so that they appeared identical to any other 10th division paratrooper. The leopard uniforms that had been specially designed for the paratroopers in Algeria were rather becoming. We had the tailors tighten the pants, because they were cut too wide, to make them look fashionable and every soldier in other military units in Algeria was envious of our uniforms. The paratroopers had to be flamboyant to better demoralize the FLN and reassure the civilian population and the camouflage uniforms provided, strangely enough, a successful ingredient.

Each regiment had dispatched two officers to the Prefecture. The civilian population found this out very quickly and tips began coming in almost immediately, progressively increasing in number and getting more detailed. There was a huge amount of information to be processed and we shared many items with the policemen very successfully. Most of time the denunciations were due to personal animosity; sometimes they came to us indirectly. Henri Damon, a former Jedburgh and special services veteran, provided the very first item. He had been captured and tortured by the Milice near Reims and had only been able to scream, just as we had been trained to. This drew the attention of his comrade, who was then able to shoot the Militiamen dead. Damon had helped me in 1946 in Pezoux, in the Loir-et-Cher region, when I was setting up a file of reserve officers of the *Action Service*. After that we were transferred to the main office where Damon joined the political section and I the *Action Service*.

His office was in the Boulevard Suchet and he had uncovered a gold smuggling operation run by the Soviets. A few days later two of Damon's fellow officers were murdered and he had been attacked by a man who suddenly appeared in front of him on the steps of the metro station at Rue-de-la-Pompe firing a submachine gun. Damon saved his own life by falling backwards down the stairs and jumping into an incoming metro train that coincidentally was closing its doors. However, Stalin's assassins were hot on his trail. After playing hide and seek in the corridors of the metro for a long time, and then on the train, Damon was able to call his wife from a pay phone, using a secret code they had agreed to in advance:

"My gray suit is dirty; bring me my blue suit right away."

The Service decided that even with a brand new suit Damon had better change scenery for a while and that was how he got himself transferred from Paris to Algeria. Henri Damon was wearing the uniform of an infantry captain with the paratrooper insignia he was very proud of. He had been placed in one of the innumerable fake cover units that were all over Algiers at the time. The unit in question was under the command of a Foreign Legion colonel. During the very first days of the battle, an Algerian Muslim woman walked into Damon's office to denounce her husband as an arms expert for the rebels. What she really wanted was to be rid of the man and she gave as her conditions in exchange for information a guarantee that she would become a widow. Damon had disagreed at first and then he came to see me at the Prefecture. I agreed to the deal and the operation was undertaken by Bigeard's regiment, which was responsible for the area.

Soon after Damon was given a second piece of information that came to him in an odd way. The office mail was sorted and delivered by a soldier who was very loyal but hopelessly lazy. To get the job done the soldier jumped into his jeep and disappeared for hours on end, always with the excuse he had a breakdown or was caught in traffic. Since the Colonel trusted the soldier the matter would end there. One day the soldier came to see Damon, looking distraught:

"Captain, you must arrest me."

"And why is that?"

"Because I lied about getting caught in traffic and having breakdowns. I spend all my time at the whorehouse."

"And so why do you want to go to the stockade?" said Damon, finding it funny.

"The whorehouse costs money and since I'm a good customer the madam told me one day that I could pay her with some hand grenades. I agreed. That's why you should put me in jail and nail that bitch as well."

Damon thought about it and answered:

"OK, we'll see later on. For now just keep quiet about the whole thing and do exactly as I tell you."

"And the whorehouse?"

"Keep on going there as if there were nothing wrong."

"What about the hand grenades?"

"You'll keep on giving them to the madam and tomorrow I'll give you a whole supply that should keep you banging away for quite some time. And not a word about this to the Colonel, understood?"

"Yes Captain!" answered the Legionnaire, standing at attention. He was clearly flabbergasted and very grateful.

Damon was a very clever intelligence officer and had not forgotten his British training. This time he decided to use the information directly rather than pass it along to us. He went to the supply depot and had a talk with the Colonel in charge of munitions, explaining the situation, and asking him to keep the operation secret and provide the hand grenades. With the help of a chief warrant officer whom the Colonel assigned to him, Damon took the hand grenades apart and disconnected the mechanism that delays the detonator once the linchpin is removed and the trigger is freed. He reassembled the grenades, hiding the changes under some fresh paint. The FLN knew our offensive hand grenades very well and could not easily be fooled other than by an expert. Had we sectioned off the detonator it would have become immediately apparent. Damon was no amateur and had prepared everything very carefully, throwing in some additional adulterated cartridge boxes. He wanted the legionnaire to spend some happy moments at the whorehouse. The cartridges were taken apart and you only had to remove some of the propulsive powder to ensure that the cartridge would explode inside the weapon. That kind of manipulation was part of our routine work.

The following day Damon summoned the legionnaire to his office under the guise of giving him an urgent piece of mail and instead handed him enough hand grenades and cartridges to have him spend his entire 48-hour pass in sexual bliss.

"You must hand all this over to the madam in one shot. Move into the whorehouse and remain there as long as you can, and remember you are not to distribute any of this piecemeal, understood? Once the party is over come back here and stay out of sight."

"Yes, Captain!" replied the happy legionnaire.

There was a real massacre during the next few days. A man at the Bab el-Oued market in the center of Algiers took out one of Damon's hand grenades to hurl it into the crowd. The man was blown to bits by the hand grenade that exploded around his midsection. Another FLN terrorist tried to throw a hand grenade through the open window of a house on the beach where we had a small observation post and lost his hand in the process. The regiment arrested the madam, bringing her to me, and I had her executed.

The FLN tried to seek vengeance at times but rarely attempted to attack the paratroopers. In any case they could only hit us blindly because their intelligence operation was unable to figure out how we operated. The FLN attempted to murder the unit commanders whose names appeared in the papers. That was how an attempt to kill Bigeard was organized in downtown Algiers. The murderer had a sketchy description of a well-built blond officer with blue eyes and five little parachutes as insignia on his chest. On the day he walked up to his intended victim, Bigeard was walking with Mayer. They were the same height, wore identical leopard uniforms, had fair hair with blue eyes and five stripes each. The *fellagha* hesitated for a second before deciding to shoot at both men, and his hesitation played a decisive role because Bigeard was smoking when it happened. Since neither Bigeard nor Mayer had any cigarettes they both walked into a smoke shop. The killer was waiting for them outside when a patrol pulled up. Soon after, a second death squad sent on the same mission killed a sergeant-major who vaguely resembled Bigeard.

No one ever tried anything on me. My name was never in the newspapers, I gave no interviews, avoided being photographed, and kept a very low profile. During the day I was just another very discreet bureaucrat. Apart from a few people in Massu's entourage and a handful of officers of the 10th DP, no one else knew that I was the main organizer of counter-terrorism. I didn't even walk around with a weapon during the day. I remembered Major Clauson in Indochina who was quite a special character when he was in command of the 1st Shock battalion. I had been impressed by the fact that he would always repeat that he didn't need to carry a gun when he was with his unit and I followed his example. Even at the headquarters of the 10th DP many officers didn't understand what was really going on. Godard's attitude had kept them apart from the hard core of the repressive units and they resented that isolation. Massu told me one day:

"You know that Le Mire is complaining that he's not participating in the battle of Algiers. Can you find something for him to do?"

"I'll think about it, General," I answered evasively.

Henri Le Mire was in charge of the 2nd Bureau of the division that dealt mostly with cartography and geographic intelligence and was assisted by Captain Jean Graziani. Since Godard had refused to get the high command involved, the staff officers were practically idle. A colonel who was in charge of military security came to the office a few days later.

"Well," he mumbled nervously. "It's about the FLN people you're arresting. We must assume, unfortunately, that later on we'll probably hear from some of them once again. They could even become important people, you understand.

So we should think of the future. Could you give us the files and the list of names?"

Garcet and I looked at each other, very puzzled by the request.

"But of course, Colonel," I answered with a broad smile. "Of course we shall be glad to oblige."

I had just had an idea. I saw Massu the next day and told him that I had found a job for Le Mire. Garcet and I went to pay Le Mire a visit and told him what he and his deputy, Graziani, would have to do to take part in the battle of Algiers.

"So I'm told you're bored and want to make yourself useful?" I asked Le Mire.

"Oh yes, that's true. We're really bored to tears!" said Graziani.

"That's great, because I've got a mission for you both."

"Excellent!"

"It's very simple: we'll give you the complete lists of the people we're placing under arrest. You'll copy the lists and hand them over to military security. But you have to be careful not to make any mistakes. There are several categories of suspects in custody."

"Oh yes? Which ones?" asked Le Mire.

"There are some suspects we don't keep. We can't hold on to everyone, you understand?"

"What do you mean?"

"That they are no longer being held as prisoners."

"And so where are they?"

"They're dead."

"Oh yes, I see."

"So in order to avoid any mistakes for those who are dead, we'll place a mark next to their names. We won't put

'D'—that would be too obvious. We'll use 'LL' as in 'liberated,' you understand?"

"Yes, fine, but what about those who are not dead and are really set free?"

"Well, for them we'll put 'FF' as in 'free.'"

Le Mire and Graziani were very busy and quiet for some time. Jean Graziani was rather desperate because paperwork was not his best subject; he clearly would have preferred some action to that kind of drudgery. He was a *pied-noir* of Corsican origin who had served with the SAS in England and had parachuted into France. He had seen action in Indochina as an officer in the 3rd Battalion of colonial paratroopers that had been wiped out on the RC4 road and his four years as a prisoner of the Viet Minh hadn't made him very soft-hearted. In 1956 he was transferred to the 6th RPC in Morocco.

There was a Communist Party meeting place in a small house in the town his regiment was garrisoned in, in Morocco. The house was promptly obliterated by an explosion. Graziani boasted to his commanding officer, Colonel Romain-Desfossés, that he had placed the bomb. Romain-Desfossés was not pleased and asked Graziani to stop. But the Communists rebuilt their house and Graziani felt that was a provocation. So he blew the house up once again. Romain-Desfossés had to call his friend Massu, whom he'd met in Africa before World War II, and ask that he take the turbulent officer into his unit. That was how Graziani had wound up in the 2nd Bureau where he was wilting alongside Le Mire with nothing to do. The colonel who was in charge of military security paid us another visit at the Prefecture, still looking puzzled. Garcet tried to avert his face to avoid laughing.

"I really don't understand what's going on," he said. "Le Mire and Graziani brought me a list with names but it looks like they've gone crazy. Most of the suspects on the list are marked as having been freed. I can't understand it, since those who are not freed are marked as being 'liberated.' I asked them to explain further but they got confused. One of them said that you asked them to mark down as 'freed' all those who were dead while the other was saying that you ordered to mark them as being 'liberated.' That's not very logical."

"You're absolutely right. It's not logical at all. There must be a misunderstanding," I answered, keeping a straight face.

A typical street inside the Casbah of Algiers.

above
November 1954, the rebellion begins and France reacts as Interior Minister François Mitterrand proclaims on radio that "Algeria is France."

right
The leaders of the FLN pose together days before the first attacks. Seated left: Krim Belkacem and at the right Larbi Ben M'Hidi.

Messali Hadj, the perennial Algerian nationalist leader,
head of the MNA, a rival party of the FLN in 1954.

Prime Minister Pierre Mendès-France (left) and
Interior Minister François Mitterrand, November, 1954.

Habib Bourguiba, Tunisian president after independence in 1956.

King Mohamed V of Morocco and
Habib Bourguiba, President of Tunisia.

Prime Minister Edgar Faure (right) with Jacques Soustelle,
Governor General of Algeria, in 1955.

above

Socialist party leader Guy Mollet was Prime Minister from January 1956 to May 1957.

right

Ferhat Abbas, long-time moderate nationalist, became president of the Algerian Provisional Government of the FLN.

Robert Lacoste was appointed by Guy Mollet to be Minister Resident in Algeria, a post he kept from February 1956 to May 1958.

General Jacques Massu, commander in Algiers from 1956 to 1960.

right

Cairo, Egypt, 1955, Ahmed Ben Bella (left) and Egyptian President Gamal Abdel Nasser were all smiles.

below

August 20, 1955: the news of the massacres of Kehnifra and Oued Zem in Morocco and Philippeville, in Algeria, where hundreds were massacred on the same day.

« Le gouvernement entend
que la répression de ces crimes
soit poursuivie
avec intransigeance »
(déclaration du président Edgar FAURE)

L'ÉCHO D'ALGER

DIMANCHE-LUNDI
21-22
Août
1955

15 FRANCS

Le plus fort tirage de l'Afrique du Nord   Directeur général : Alain de SÉRIGNY   Trois éditions quotidiennes

Entre KHENIFRA et OUED-ZEM
**Trois journalistes français
sont tués dans une embuscade**
(INFORMATION EN PAGE 4)

Visant **Constantine, Philippeville** et de nombreux centres du Nord constantinois

Un sanglant mouvement insurrectionnel
déclenché samedi à midi
est écrasé en quelques heures

800 rebelles avaient entraîné avec eux
plus de **3.000 fellahs** fanatisés
Les forces de l'ordre mises en état d'alerte
ont réagi avec rapidité et efficacité

Devant l'assaut des rebelles fanatisés

PHILIPPEVILLE
et sa région ont vécu
des heures horribles

**Les parachutistes ont rétabli la situation
dans l'après-midi, après avoir dû faire
le siège de véritables « fort Chabrol »**

La ville assaillie
par les rebelles

BILAN PROVISOIRE
ÉTABLI HIER SOIR

**475 cadavres
de hors-la-loi
dénombrés
800 prisonniers**

69 tués et 156 blessés
civils et militaires

Au Maroc de graves émeutes
ont ensanglanté Khenifra et Oued-Zem

Les grands centres urbains
ont été relativement calmes

René JANON, notre envoyé spécial
était samedi à OUED-ZEM

**"Partout la mort
et la désolation
sur mes lèvres expire
une espèce de sanglot"**

Plus de cent cinquante morts
européens (civils et militaires)

LE BILAN PROVISOIRE
par région
DES ÉVÉNEMENTS

above
The mining village at El-Halia, near Philippeville.

below
Bodies of children massacred at El-Halia.

Zighoud Youssef, the rebel leader who gave instructions
to be particularly cruel at El-Halia and Philippeville.
He was later killed in a firefight with paratroopers.

left

Colonel Ducourneau, the first paratrooper commander during the early stages of the Algerian war.

below

Dead FLN fighters at the stadium at Philippeville in August, 1955.

General Raoul Salan, supreme commander of
the French army in Algeria from 1956 to 1959.

Robert Lacoste (right) with Max Lejeune, Secretary of the Armed Forces in the government of Guy Mollet.

FLN leaders ready to board an Air Maroc DC3 at Rabat airport are seen off by crown prince Moulay Hassan (in uniform). They never reached their destination in Tunis.

FLN leaders in the paddy wagon under arrest at Algiers airport.
Ahmed Ben Bella is at the extreme left.

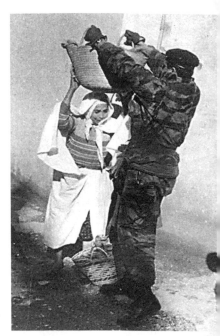

right and below
French paratroopers conduct
anti-terrorist searches.

Fernand Yveton, caught with a
bomb in October 1956, was executed
in February 1957.

Larbi Ben M'Hidi under arrest by Bigeard's men
after the failure of the general strike.

Larbi Ben M'Hidi was summarily executed by hanging by General Aussaresses himself.

Paratroopers in charge of public safety take
a census of the population of the Casbah.

Maurice Bourgès-Maunoury,
Prime Minister from May to November 1957.

above
Colonel Roger Trinquier, part of
General Massu's staff in 1957 with
General Aussaresses, a major at the time.

right
Colonel Jeanpierre, the legendary
paratrooper leader who died in combat.

left

Colonel Yves Godard became the head of intelligence on Massu's staff after Aussaresses left in the summer of 1957.

below

The paratrooper leaders (from the left): Fossey-François, Mayer, Bigeard, Massu, Godard, Brothier, and Jeanpierre. Aussaresses was never photographed during this period.

Yacef Saadi, the baker of the Casbah and
main organizer of terrorism inside Algiers.

The women, recruited by Yacef Saadi, who planted the deadly bombs in Algiers seen together. (Left to right): Samia Lakhdari, Djamila Bouhired, Hassiba Bent Bouali, Zohra Drif.

Ali Amar, better known as Ali-la-Pointe.

above
Ali-la-Pointe died in the huge explosion
that devastated his hiding place.

right
Hassiba Ben Bouali, who was killed with Ali-la-Pointe.

above
Germaine Tillion, the liberal French anthropologist
who had a private meeting with Yacef Saadi.

right
Zora Drif under arrest in Algiers.

below
The city of Algiers in 1957.

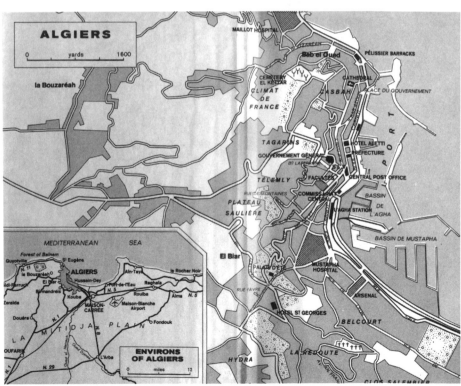

General de Gaulle during an inspection with
Colonel Trinquier in 1959.

11

The Bazooka

I was out with my men as usual on the night of January
16-17, 1957. During my rounds I dropped in at the Villa
Sésini, which was the command center of the 1st REP.
"Borniol"* was on duty that night. That was the nickname
everyone used when referring to Lieutenant Jean-Marie Le
Pen, the squad leader of one of the combat companies, because of funeral duties he had to carry out during the Suez
operation just a few weeks before. The Egyptians had many

---

* The name "Borniol" is well known throughout France as the
largest undertaker in the country.

losses and their dead littered the roads in the desert heat. Massu had ordered Colonel Brothier, who was in command of the 1st REP, to get rid of the bodies and Le Pen's squad was handed that unenviable task. Le Pen had performed very well as undertaker and hadn't forgotten any of the special attention due to those soldiers of the Muslim faith. He ordered some prisoners to dig a huge ditch, making sure it would allow the bodies to face Mecca, and even went so far as to take the dead men's shoes off.

Le Pen was very scrupulous when he was on duty, but if he was not in action—which was very rarely the case—he had a reputation for being rather rough. I was told that he enjoyed starting fights in the most elegant spots in town. Whenever he was at his favorite spot at the trendy bar of the Saint George Hotel, where most European celebrities came to visit, he could be seen frequently picking a fight with anyone whose looks he didn't like, to the chagrin of Thomas, the Armenian bartender. I usually avoided the Saint George, but for reasons no one in Algiers would have figured out. By a strange coincidence my father had been friendly with one of the founders of the hotel when he was a student and the Aussaresses name was now among the main shareholders of the corporation that owned the place. I had often heard my father complain about what a bad investment the hotel had been and the fact that his partners didn't pay him his fair share of the profits. That was the reason why I avoided the place and preferred the Aletti, which was much less fashionable.

But the reason "Borniol" and I were on a first-name basis was not because we spent time at the same waterholes but because we had both been part of the Catholic Student

Organization. Le Pen appeared very surprised to see that I wasn't talking about the day's main event.

"Don't you know what's happened?"

"What would that be?" I asked.

"Well, what happened to the big boss, or rather what was intended for the boss because he was spared by a matter of seconds?"

"Who do you mean? Massu?"

"No, Salan!"

"What happened?"

Le Pen started laughing.

"I'm amazed you don't know about this! Well, you're certainly in good shape for someone who is supposedly the best informed person in Algiers!"

That's how Jean-Marie Le Pen told me about what had taken place. Using a very rudimentary set of pipes, two rockets had been fired at the office window of General Raoul Salan, the commander in chief and commander of the military region in Algeria. Salan was unscathed but his staff officer, Major Rodier, had been killed. A few hours later at a secret morning meeting, Massu opened the proceedings by attacking us. Trinquier kept silent.

"So this is the way you're handling the *fellagha*?" asked Massu.

"General, this incident is completely outside our mission!" I answered.

"What do you mean not part of your mission? Aren't your orders to get rid of those who are attacking us?"

"Yes, to stop FLN-sponsored attacks."

"So?"

"The FLN isn't behind this attack."

"And how do you know that?"

"Because the FLN can't handle the kind of technology that was used in this case. I'm ready to vouch for that."

Massu grumbled and thought for a while.

"So who could have done this?" he finally asked.

"I think it looks more like the Reds, but we have to investigate it further."

The investigation was handed over to the criminal police department.

On January 18 I met with Police Superintendent Parat and was introduced on that occasion to Honoré Gévaudan, who had been dispatched from Paris to assist Parat in the investigation. Gévaudan had already been active in Algiers in 1956 when we were looking for the team set up by Yveton, the Communist gas company employee who had conspired with a *pied-noir* chemist to blow up the city. Gévaudan later told me that they had to use torture to force Yveton to talk, in spite of the fact that Paul Teitgen had expressly forbidden it, for fear of risking the destruction of twenty-five percent of Algiers itself. Gévaudan was talking to Faulques, the intelligence officer of the 1st REP when I told them what I thought of the case.

"So you think this is a Red plot?" asked Gévaudan.

"It's one possible explanation. I have no proof. I'm basing it on intuition, as a possibility."

"But who could it be among the Reds?"

"I'm thinking of their Action Service, the team led by André Moine," I answered.

They all nodded, looking at each other.

"It makes sense," said Gévaudan.

The following day when I met with Massu, we discussed the problem once more.

"What's this story about the Communist Action Service?" he asked.

"I feel the Communists have something similar to our *Action Service*. What I mean is that they have a secret commando unit that includes weapons and explosives experts. André Moine heads that unit."

"Who is he?"

"Moine is a former labor organizer in charge of violent operations for the Communist Party. It wouldn't be the first time communists are involved in attacks of this nature. There was the weapon used in the October 6 attack, where you were the target, which was a Sten submachine gun that was part of the weapons supply stolen by Second Lieutenant Maillot. Then there is Yveton and a year and a half ago I found the *fellagha* hiding in Communist Party offices in Philippeville."

"So why are you waiting to arrest this André Moine?"

I began doing some research on the PCA, which frightened its leadership, driving them underground. Some of them were to resurface only in June of that year. Parat and Gévaudan were making headway on their end and it was to be a very ordinary policeman of the scientific unit who uncovered the mystery. The perpetrators of the attack had left their weapons at the location they had used and those supplies were to give them away. In analyzing the electrical wire used to detonate the trigger the lab technician noticed that it had fourteen wires instead of the ordinary nineteen; he traced its origin to an electrician who was employed at the arsenal. He was a *pied-noir* who had served in Indochina and readily admitted his deed when they questioned him. Parat and Gévaudan had been influenced by what I had said and were convinced the man was a Communist. But the man felt so insulted at being mistaken as a member of the group he hated the most that he preferred to come clean, telling the whole story.

Since he was an excellent swimmer, he had been accepted as a member of a very exclusive sports club organized by Doctor Kovacs. A man named Philippe Castille was also a club member and was placed under arrest a few days later. He was the perpetrator of the attack. My suspicion targeting the Algerian Communist Party was unfounded. When I discovered that Philippe Castille was involved I was completely amazed. Many things have been said and written about the attempt to kill Salan, even that it had been organized by French intelligence or by Israel. I had been Philippe Castille's instructor at the 11th Shock battalion for training on the bazooka and knew him quite well even though I hadn't seen him in a long time.

At Montlouis we had been supplied with hundreds of weapons, including Panzerfaust rocket launchers captured from the Germans, but there were no manuals on how to handle them. So we had taken them apart and Castille became an expert at it until one day we were told that some Panzerfausts could have been cleverly booby-trapped. We therefore had to destroy them all.

Castille and his parents had been active in the Resistance. Because of a personnel cutback Castille hadn't stayed at Saint-Cyr, where he had been admitted, and the former Boy Scout was transferred to the 11th Shock where he reported to me. After that he married a girl from a well-to-do family from around Perpignan and got himself a good job working for Renault in Algiers. He became friendly with Doctor Kovacs, who had served as a medical officer in an infantry battalion during the Italian campaign. Kovacs won Castille over to his political ideas. They were both wrongly convinced that because Salan was, notoriously, a member of the Freemasons he would sooner or later be in favor of giving independence to Algeria. Kovacs wanted to use a 24-29 automatic rifle to murder Salan but Castille was able to prove that was absurd and that the best weapon would be an offshoot of the Panzerfaust, which he knew very well. That was how Castille had manufactured the weapon with the help of two workmen at the arsenal.

Castille had been very careful in planning the attack. He rented a room in a house in front of the building Salan was using as his headquarters and spent a lot of time observing the General's movements and habits. The operation started just when Salan had unexpectedly left his office to meet with Robert Lacoste. Since he used an underpass, Castille didn't see him leaving the building and thought Salan was still inside. When Major Rodier, Salan's chief of staff, sat in his boss' armchair to have a meeting with a Colonel, Castille was convinced the General had returned and triggered the firing pin of both rockets. One rocket went over the Colonel's head while he was sitting facing the desk and the shell had cut through Rodier, to wind up at the feet of another officer. That was how Rodier lost his life, because he made the mistake of sitting in his commanding officer's armchair.

During his trial in 1958 Castille was nice enough to never mention me or his stint at the 11th Shock. His lawyer advised him to accuse Kovacs, who had fled to Spain and whom I didn't know. But that was not the kind of thing Castille would do and he served twelve years in prison instead. After some three years in jail, Castille and his two accomplices were hospitalized. In January 1960, during the week of the barricades in Algiers, while there was some confusion he decided with his friends to escape from the hospital and return to France. They went to the bistro *L'Ile-de-Beauté*, but the two workers returned to the hospital. Castille managed to go to France where he became the leader of the plastic bombers of the OAS. By joining the OAS he also became friendly with General Salan, the man he had wanted to kill. In 1962 Castille was arrested by Honoré Gévaudan once again just as he was about to blow up the television transmitter on top of the Eiffel tower at the start of a speech by General de Gaulle. This time he was sentenced to twenty years of hard labor. After failing to escape, Philippe Castille was freed in 1968 from the penitentiary at Saint-Martin-de-Ré, where he spent 6 years and discovered a new interest in stained glass art.

12

The Strike

A s I mentioned earlier during our very first conversation on January 8, 1957, Massu had asked me to help break the insurrectional strike that had been announced for January 28 in the leaflets signed by Ben M'Hidi. For three weeks non-stop I worked on the files obtained from the RG. The Beni-Messous camp now held about 1,500 prisoners while the others had been shipped out to other smaller camps. Many suspects had been questioned and most of them had been involved in the bloody attacks that continued to hit everyone very hard. On Saturday, January 26, three bombs exploded at once in some bistros in the rue Michelet:

the Otomatic, the Cafeteria, and the Coq-Hardi. The one at the Coq-Hardi was the worst, with four women dead and thirty-seven people wounded.

We were able to arrest many of the people who had set the bombs, as well as their lieutenants, but we hadn't been able to arrest anyone among the leaders of the strike. I didn't want to show how worried we were by the strike and eager and capable of breaking it. The FLN was therefore not expecting the army's reaction. I knew that the rebels could paralyze public services and I was determined to make sure these were able to function in all circumstances. During the battle of Algiers, the FLN was so powerful that no area could be considered as being out of its reach. It was therefore difficult even to trust the mail or the telephone.

During the night of January 27-28, 1957 I made the rounds of the regiments to make sure that they were ready for action. I had assigned a specific responsibility of one public utility—water, gas, electricity, postal service, trolley cars, etc.—to each individual employee who was on the lists provided to us by the personnel services. Those lists were compared systematically to the new files we had set up after questioning suspects. At dawn the paratroopers took positions in every area where the people employed by a public utility were supposed to go. They carefully checked who had reported for work and who had not. Then they quickly visited the homes of the strikers and dragged them rather roughly, as may be imagined, to their jobs. Thanks to such drastic methods public utilities were running again very early in the morning. The preparation and execution of such an operation in a city of 800,000 was a gigantic task.

This action was a spectacular demonstration of the strength of our units and the psychological effect was that we were able to break the strike in less than one hour. The doors of closed stores were torn open and the retailers who had been informed of what they were risking had to rush to their shops for fear of being looted. I was supervising these operations from the Prefecture when a French civilian who was in the management of the organization of maritime freight forwarders came to see me. He told me that the long-shoremen were on strike and that it was a disaster and something had to be done. I ran over to the Beni-Messous camp to find some help. With a chief warrant officer we assembled 200 men and marched them over to the port of Algiers under escort of some young paratrooper sapper draftees—combat engineers. The men unloaded the ships twice as fast as the longshoremen and the harbormaster insisted on paying wages to the prisoners. Everyone was pleased with the outcome.

Once the unloading operation was completed I returned to the Prefecture around noon. I intended to have a quick lunch at the *Ile-de-Beauté* restaurant but as I crossed the square a young lieutenant in the Foreign Legion invited me to the mess hall. I was amazed to notice that the waiters were on strike. A loud noise was building up in the main hall, where we were sitting, at the table of two sisters from Brittany whom I knew from the women's infantry corps. They were rather sarcastic when they saw us:

"Well, you paratroopers can certainly be proud of this situation. You couldn't even stop the waiters in the mess hall from going on strike! We're wondering how things are shaping up elsewhere. This is nothing to write home about."

A waiter was walking with a smirk on his face around the tables and I stopped him:

"So what's all this shit about? What are you waiting for to serve us?"

"I'm on strike."

"What did you say?"

The entire mess hall fell silent.

"I'm telling you that I'm on strike and won't serve you. I can't help it if you don't like that."

I got up suddenly. The waiter was looking at me with a smile. So I slapped him. Both his colleagues and he went right back to work. At the end of the meal the maitre d' came over, saying that the manager would like to see me. Since I didn't pay him the honor of my visit he went to headquarters and complained about me to Colonel Thomazo, whom everyone called "Leather Nose" (because of his broken nose the Colonel had to wear a leather strap across his face). I was even called in and Thomazo, being in command of the mess, wanted to put me in the stockade for eight days. I refused to sign the papers and told him in no uncertain terms what I thought about his mess hall and walked out. Colonel Mayer tore up the request for my punishment. My men and the regimental lieutenants wanted to slit Thomazo's throat and blame it on the FLN once they heard about the incident. I tried to quiet them down but they still managed to go to the mess hall and raise hell. After that, all the officers of the 1st RCP were banned from using the mixed mess hall in central Algiers.

On January 29, the second day of the strike, every public service employee reported to work. Everyone felt that the paratroopers were watching them. A few stores were still closed, mostly by those who had been forced to open and had to clean up the mess inside. The paratroopers were diligently identifying the strike leaders. We targeted mostly businesses and all those who had no reason being there were automatically marched off. We questioned the workers at construction sites:

"Why aren't you working?"

"We're on strike."

"And why are you on strike?"

"Well, because we were told to go on strike."

"And who told you that?"

"People we don't know."

"People from the FLN?"

"Maybe."

At that point we would suddenly ask for identity documents and crosschecked everyone. Whenever we ran into someone who had no business being at the site, for instance a barber, it was clear that such a person was an FLN cadre who had come to impart orders to the strikers. Those suspects were taken away for questioning. For the most part the strike that was to turn into an insurrection was a complete fiasco for the FLN.

13

Villa des Tourelles

The battle of Algiers took place at night. Control of the night of Algiers was the prize we had to retake from the FLN. It was easy to imagine that the secret and nightly character of my mission was to organize the arrests, sort out the suspects, supervise the questioning, and the summary executions. Even though it wasn't spelled out in so many words, the more observant people understood that my job was to unburden the regiments of the most unpalatable tasks and to cover those they had to undertake on their own. If any problem were to crop up the heat would have automatically been placed upon me. The regimental intelligence officers knew it as much as I did.

The only person I was seeing on a daily basis who never really understood any of it was Paul Teitgen. This was very surprising because he was a rather smart man and also because the people he reported to and his colleagues in the Prefecture were also in the know.

Garcet quickly located a discreet building we could use in the Mustapha district in the suburbs of Algiers. It was a large two-story structure with four rooms on each floor, and a cellar surrounded by an unkempt garden. The house had a fated name: villa des Tourelles, which was the same name as the barracks in Paris where the headquarters of the SDECE was located. The DGSE, the new name of the intelligence service, is still located at the *"caserne des Tourelles."* The villa was in a rather isolated area, which was to our advantage since there were no neighbors close by who could interfere with our task. At that location we would question the prisoners who were assigned to us. We spent the day at the offices of the Prefecture, but after that we would rush over to the Tourelles, as we called it.

Before sundown I quickly compiled the information coming in from the various regiments and made decisions about problems of territorial responsibility. Then Garcet and I would get ready for the operations of that night, which never required very complicated preparations. The regiments were given those tasks that required more planning. The main issue was to evaluate the risks involved in each operation. If they were not dangerous I would give Lieutenant Garcet my instructions and he would handle the matter with my first group or even with only a single man to help him.

For example, an Algerian walked into the Prefecture and had a meeting with Garcet. The man had married a French woman who had left him to live with an FLN sympathizer, who dressed like a dandy and was involved with other men who were planting bombs. The following night, two of my men went to the address we had been given. When we saw one of the men return to the villa wearing a brand new but slightly tight fitting suit, the kind that only a ladies' man would wear, we knew the operation had taken place. My men found the suspect, who had a closet full of expensive clothes. Since he confessed to everything on the spot, the men thought that it was unnecessary to even drive him back to the villa.

At sunset we slipped into our leopard camouflage uniforms and the horse race would begin. Our team would start at 8 p.m. and we'd be sure to return before midnight with the suspects to proceed with the questioning. Throughout the night the regiments kept me informed of the arrests they were making and often would wait for me to arrive to decide the fate of the prisoners. I was responsible for the decisions regarding all the suspects arrested inside the city of Algiers—as to those who should be interrogated immediately and those who were to be sent directly to the camps because they were less important to us. The latter was the case for people with a weak link to the FLN or who had been forced to join. This was the vast majority of the suspects we apprehended.

We would hold on to the others who were either positively dangerous or thought to be so and make them talk quickly before executing them. At times I was running from one regimental headquarters to another and at other times I would go along with one of my two groups to make arrests when the operation appeared sensitive or very risky. There were fewer than ten of us using the big car, two jeeps and two Dodge pick-ups. We traveled very fast, always racing for time. The nights were never long enough for us.

The suspects we took directly were those under the jurisdiction of several sectors or under no sector at all. This was always the case if they were located outside the city of Algiers. Most operations we would undertake and that I took part in would end in questioning. Others ended in straightforward executions done on the spot. I remember some women who had accused certain men of being murderers. The culprits were hiding in a shack near the Zeralda forest, located within Colonel Fossey-François' sector. We didn't bother questioning the men and they were executed then and there. We never handled more than half a dozen suspects at any one time. The mere fact that they were at the villa des Tourelles meant they were considered so dangerous that they were not to get out of there alive. These were men who had directly participated in deadly attacks.

At the same time each regiment of the 10th DP was proceeding with its own interrogations of the suspects it had arrested. If the information the regiments came by went beyond their territorial sector, they would send the prisoner to me and I would question him again. For example, if Bigeard's men arrested someone who had information about the sector of Maison-Carrée, a location under Mayer's control, the prisoner was passed on to me. On very heavy days I would get all those the regiments could not handle or didn't have time to question.

We began the interrogations as quickly as the suspects were brought in. At the villa des Tourelles, just as for all the regiments that were responsible for other sectors, torture was used as a matter of course if the prisoner refused to talk, which was a common occurrence. The information we obtained would sometimes lead us to take another trip our- selves, for instance to find an arms or explosives cache. Oth- erwise we would ask local units to proceed with new arrests.

When we had to go back out to check on the informa- tion we had obtained, the prisoners were left under the guard of a single man who stayed behind at the villa. Once a pris- oner had talked or appeared to have nothing more to say, the worst we could do to him was to set him free on the spot. It would happen if a prisoner had me promise to free him if he talked. But that rarely happened. Once outside, the man was practically guaranteed to have his throat slit by the FLN before dawn.

Most of the time my men traveled about twenty kilome- ters outside Algiers to some "remote location" where the suspects were shot with submachine guns and then buried. Executions were never held in the same spot twice. I asked my deputy, Garcet, to pick the men for the job. I was also handed additional unwanted prisoners who had been ques- tioned by other units and had talked. In such cases no one ever asked me what I intended to do with them. So, when they wanted to get rid of somebody he would wind up at the villa des Tourelles.

At the end of each night I wrote down the events that had taken place in a top-secret notebook called the "mani- fold," which made four carbon copies at once. The original was sent to General Massu, one copy to the minister in resi- dence for Algeria, Robert Lacoste, one copy to General Salan, and the third copy for my files. I obviously kept that note- book on me at all times.

In my report I would compile all the information I had received during the night from each intelligence officer. I noted the number of arrests made by each unit, the number of suspects who had been shot during arrest, the number of summary executions undertaken by my group or by the regiments. I rarely made notes of any names except when I thought it was of some importance. I almost never slept, two hours at the most at the end of the night, and a one-hour nap during the day. Since I was not a smoker I kept awake by drinking gallons of coffee. A draftee was assigned as the driver of my jeep, which I used most of the time. One night he fell asleep at the wheel and we crashed off the road. An officer of the automotive division at headquarters had us stop to rest while all his mechanics went to work on the vehicle. By dawn the jeep was as good as new.

Every morning after a last cup of coffee I would have a meeting with Trinquier and pay a visit to Massu at Hydra to inform him of what had happened. He would see us secretly at his home so that we would have no contact with divisional officers. Trinquier and I both knew that Massu would meet with Lacoste immediately following his meeting with us. In handing Massu his copy of the "manifold" sheet I'd also give him some quick explanations about the conduct of the operations. The executions of prisoners were often listed as aborted escape attempts. I tried to avoid giving Massu too much time to think and become uneasy.

In a sort of unwritten code in such instances Massu would only grunt his reaction, which couldn't be interpreted as being either congratulatory or disapproving. But he would unfailingly cover his subordinates in every instance and that was a great quality of his. The meetings between Massu, Trinquier, and myself took place daily. We tried to limit our meetings with the various regimental commanders who tended to act like prima donnas when they were all together. Each commander would inevitably announce his results with pride, hoping to best his rivals. During the spring someone even had the silly idea of making a tally of the weapons captured from the FLN by each unit. That system of tallying successes contributed to creating even more childish rivalry, which was completely unacceptable. I remembered that in Indochina such a system had been tried before and one regiment had put in a toy gun, calling it an instructional weapon captured from the enemy. I could see that we would soon reach that kind of level in Algiers.

Every day I also sent a separate report to Teitgen, listing all the persons under arrest by name. For each name he had to sign an official order placing the person under house arrest. I am sure that Teitgen had always known that the most important suspects whose names were on the list were being tortured. He probably didn't know that after the torture they were also executed, unless he was pretending not to know. On March 29, 1957 Teitgen handed in his resignation in a long letter he addressed to Robert Lacoste, in which he stated that he had personally seen prisoners bearing the signs of physical torture. Lacoste refused to accept his resignation.

14

The Terror

By asking the military to reestablish law and order inside the city of Algiers, the civilian authorities had implicitly approved of having summary executions. Whenever we felt it was necessary to be given more explicit instructions, the practice in question was always clearly approved. At the end of January 1957, the 3rd RPC under the command of Marcel Bigeard captured some twelve expert killers, known as the "Notre-Dame d'Afrique" group. They had been associated with several attacks involving French citizens and Algerians. Bigeard told me that he didn't know what to do with them.

I talked to Trinquier about the matter and the following day we were to have a meeting of regimental commanders at the division level. Suddenly, during the meeting, Bigeard brought up a problem that was on his mind:

"So what should I do with those guys?"

"Maybe they should be let loose in the countryside," answered Trinquier.

"Yes and be sure the countryside is far away," said Massu.

Everyone understood what he meant.

"Just wait a little while, though," continued the General, "because we're about to welcome Max Lejeune, who's coming to pay us a visit. I'll talk to him about this and it'll be a good opportunity to see what kind of man he is."

During his private meeting with Max Lejeune, Massu told him that a group of terrorists had been arrested and that he was hesitating as to whether they should be handed over to the justice system or simply executed.

"Do you remember the DC-3 of *Air-Atlas*, the plane that was carrying Ben Bella, the head of the FLN, and his four companions last October 22?" asked Max Lejeune.

"Who wouldn't remember something like that, Mr. Minister," answered Massu.

"It's a matter I'm well acquainted with because Premier Guy Mollet had me sort it out with General Lorillot. Once the government found out that those men were flying from Morocco to Tunisia, orders were given to the fighter planes based in Oran to shoot the plane down. The only reason we cancelled the order was that at the last minute we found out that the pilot and crew were French. It's regrettable for the French government that Ben Bella should still be alive. His arrest was a mistake. We intended to kill him."

Massu understood the message Max Lejeune was giving him. He summoned Trinquier and me immediately. When he told us that anecdote, the message was crystal clear for me as well: I would be executing twelve more men the following night. I could have left that unsavory task for Bigeard to finish but I preferred doing it myself with the NCOs of my first team. When we killed those prisoners there was no doubt in our minds that we were following the direct orders of Max Lejeune, who was part of the government of Guy Mollet, and acting in the name of the French Republic.

Only rarely were the prisoners we had questioned during the night still alive the next morning. Whether they had talked or not they generally had been neutralized. It was impossible to send them back to the court system, there were too many of them and the machine of justice would have become clogged with cases and stopped working altogether. Furthermore, many of the prisoners would probably have managed to avoid any kind of punishment.

I was well aware of this because every morning I visited the main camp at Beni-Messous where I would meet with Police Superintendent Ceccaldi-Raynaud and his deputy, Inspector Devichi. We had to proceed with a new filtering of suspects at that time. Among those under house arrest, some were assigned to the judicial system. This was my area and I had to make the decision that same day. About 20,000 people had gone through that camp, representing three percent of the entire population of Algiers. How could we expect the justice system to accommodate all these people?

During one of my visits Devichi had pointed out a prisoner who hadn't been questioned and who he felt sure was part of the FLN. The suspect understood that we were talking about him and I could notice that he was in a panic. Devichi and I agreed that I would handle the case later on. After I left the camp the prisoner went up to the police officer in charge and admitted having committed several murders. He was then incarcerated according to the regular procedure at the prison of Algiers, and when questioned by the judge told him a very implausible story. After investigation the only crime that this man could be accused of was of having insulted a public official, which led to his being set free. By accusing himself of a string of murders that he hadn't committed he had been able to get out of the camp.

The justice system would have been paralyzed had it not been for our initiative. Many terrorists would have been freed and given the opportunity of launching other attacks. Even if the law had been enforced in all its harshness, few persons would have been executed. The judicial system was not suited for such drastic conditions. Even if Mitterrand, who was then minister of justice, had handed terrorist cases in Algeria over to military courts it would still have not been enough. Sending prisoners who had committed murder to wait in camps for the judiciary to hear their cases was also impossible because many would have escaped during transfers with the help of the FLN.

Summary executions were therefore an inseparable part of the tasks associated with keeping law and order. That was the reason why the army had been called in. Counter-terrorism had been instituted, but obviously only unofficially. Clearly we had to wipe out the FLN and only the army had the tools for the task. It was so obvious that it became unnecessary to spell out such orders at any level.

No one ever asked me openly to execute this one or that one. It was simply understood.

Regarding the use of torture, it was tolerated if not actually recommended. François Mitterrand, as minister of justice, had a de facto representative with General Massu in Judge Jean Bérard, who covered our actions and knew exactly what was going on during the night. I had an excellent relationship with him, with nothing to hide.

While torture was widely used in Algeria, it didn't mean that it was an ordinary occurrence. We didn't discuss it among officers and an interrogation didn't necessarily end up in torture. Some prisoners started talking very easily. Others only needed some roughing up. It was only when a prisoner refused to talk or denied the obvious that torture was used. We did everything we possibly could to avoid having the youngest soldiers bloody their hands and many would have been unable to see it through anyway. The methods I used were always the same: beatings, electric shocks, and, in particular, water torture, which was the most dangerous technique for the prisoner. It never lasted for more than one hour and the suspects would speak in the hope of saving their own lives. They would therefore either talk quickly or never.

Massu decided to undergo electric shock torture himself in order to reassure his men. He was right in a sense: if you have neither experienced nor been subjected to torture, it's impossible to talk about it. But Massu was not crazy and he had carefully picked his torturers among his most devoted courtiers. Had I been doing the torturing he would have been subjected to the exact same treatment as the one we handed to the suspects. He would have remembered and would have understood that torture is much more unpleasant to the victim than to the torturer.

I don't think I ever tortured or executed people who were innocent. I was mainly dealing with terrorists who had been involved in attacks. It must be remembered that for every bomb, whether or not it had exploded, there was a chemist, a bomb maker, a driver, a lookout, and a terrorist who set the detonator. Up to twenty people each time. In my view the responsibility of each one of the accomplices was overwhelming, even though the perpetrators may have thought that they were merely the links in a long chain.

Prisoners would rarely die during an interrogation but it did happen. I remember a man, an Arab about forty who was very thin. We had arrested him after a denunciation. Outwardly he looked like an honest laborer but he was suspected of having manufactured bombs and every clue pointed in that direction. Naturally he adamantly denied everything. He claimed to have tuberculosis, that he would not have known how to make a bomb and that he didn't even know what that was. It was true that he had a pension because of a pulmonary disease but what he didn't know was that when we searched his house we found some schneiderite (an explosive commonly used by the FLN) and his military records showing that in the army he was in the engineer corps and had handled explosives. So this was how the French army wound up training an explosives expert operating quietly while on a government pension, a fair illustration of the failure of the system.

I didn't use torture. I just pulled out his military record and asked if it belonged to him. The man was taken aback when he saw the booklet. He finally admitted that on occasion he had manufactured bombs but that he was no longer doing it. I showed him the products that we found at his home. He told me that he was just a worker and didn't know what happened to the bombs once he had made them and that he was not involved in politics. He didn't arm the bombs nor did he choose the targets. He bore no responsibility. At that point I knew enough to have him executed and I would have preferred to end the questioning. But I wanted to find out who his contacts were, who gave the orders, and the targets of the bombs he had just produced. There were clues indicating that he knew several higher ups and that he had information regarding the targets that had been picked.

I was questioning him inside a small deserted hangar. I only had a tap and a water hose. The man was sitting on a chair and I was sitting in front of him. He looked at me with a defiant little smile. Once it became clear that he wouldn't talk I decided to use water and I signaled my men, who tied his hands behind his back and stuck the hose into his mouth. The man choked and struggled. He still refused to talk. He must have imagined that we would execute him anyway so he decided not to betray anyone, and he must have prepared himself for a long time for such a situation just as I had, years before, when I was going on a mission. However, I had never fought civilians and never harmed children. I was fighting men who had made their own choices.

I refused to promise him that he would be spared. That wasn't true. Even if I had set him free he was done for. He had nothing to lose. My thoughts went back to Philippeville and to the priests who came back from the mineshaft at El-Halia crying. Yet they had seen other horrors before. We had to give them some whiskey so that they would go back and pick up the body parts of the children, hoping to re-constitute the dead bodies on sheets.

"Shall we put on the handkerchief?" the soldier asked me.

"OK, put it on. But go slow."

An NCO placed the cloth on the man's face. The other soldier sprayed water over it to prevent air from getting through. They waited a few seconds. When they took off the handkerchief the man was dead.

I called in the doctor, who was an old friend of mine from my school days in Bordeaux.

"I was talking to the prisoner and he fell ill," I said unconvincingly. "He told me he had tuberculosis. Can you see what's wrong with him?"

"You were talking to him? But he's drenched. You must be kidding!" said the doctor.

"No, I wouldn't do such a thing."

"But he's dead!"

"It's possible," I answered, "but when I asked for you he was still alive."

Since the doctor was still complaining I lost my cool and said:

"And so? You want me to say that I killed him? Would that make you feel better? Do you think I enjoy this?"

"No, but then why did you come to get me if he's dead?"

I didn't answer. The doctor finally understood. I had called him so he would send the body to the hospital and get it out of my sight once and for all.

15

Ben M'Hidi

Two enormous explosions set only minutes apart went off on Sunday afternoon, February 10, 1957, in Algiers. During a soccer match two bombs had destroyed the grand stand at the municipal stadium and the El-Biar stadium, causing the deaths of eleven people and seriously wounding 146 others, who for the most part had been mutilated. The next day, while Fernand Yveton was being executed, Massu treated Trinquier and myself to a violent dressing down, as if we had both been responsible for the attacks.

"This is what I get? You bunch of no good bastards! This time you give me bombs!"

Massu was jumping to conclusions. As far as he was concerned our job was to wipe out the FLN. Therefore, if bombs were going off it was entirely our fault. We also understood our mission that way so we had no hesitations in accomplishing it vigorously. These attacks focused our determination and less than one week later during the night of February 15-16, we arrested Larbi Ben M'Hidi. We found his address, placing him in the sector under Bigeard and the 3rd RPC. The unit's intelligence officer, Jacques Allaire, was in charge of the operation. This extremely sensitive piece of information remained secret for one week.

Ben M'Hidi was undoubtedly the mastermind of all the attacks and the main protagonist in the battle of Algiers in his capacity as head of the CCE—the *Comité de coordination et d'exécution*—which had been set up to replace Ben Bella's team. Bigeard created a friendly atmosphere and made his prisoner feel very comfortable. Both men spent entire nights in private conversation and drinking coffee. Bigeard thought he could use the old rivalry that existed between Ben M'Hidi and Ben Bella. All he had to do was praise Ben Bella inordinately and pretend that Ben M'Hidi was just a temporary replacement. The prisoner then started talking without even noticing it and Bigeard played the role of the skeptic. Ben M'Hidi then became even more talkative and wound up giving away details in spite of himself, details proving that he was indeed one of the leaders of the FLN. He only spoke of an area he felt was of secondary importance, namely the supply system and the logistics used by the FLN, but his information was extremely important.

Bigeard and Ben M'Hidi would compare their troops, their systems, just like two old fighting comrades. Bigeard let himself be taken in by his own game and certainly felt a kind of friendship for the FLN leader, who was obviously never once tortured. Such a close relationship between the two men could lead to insoluble problems. Bigeard kept on repeating that they should use Ben M'Hidi and that he would find a way to convince him, but Massu didn't like the situation at all. The way Ben M'Hidi was being treated was not to everyone's liking. Massu had appointed Judge Bérard to his staff. The Judge's office was almost next door to my own and I would often see him at the Prefecture. Bérard was an examining magistrate whose mission it was to keep Minister of Justice François Mitterrand's cabinet directly informed of what we were doing, thus bypassing the prosecutor's office.

Bérard was very much excited by the arrest of Ben M'Hidi and never stopped talking about it with me.

"But what are we going to do about this Ben M'Hidi?" he asked me one morning.

"I'm not really concerned about what we're going to do with him. I didn't arrest him, it's Bigeard's responsibility not mine."

"But aren't you somewhat involved in any case?"

"Why would that be?"

"I just want to know if you proceeded to do a body search."

"I wouldn't be the one to do that."

"That's exactly what I mean. If you didn't search him, you didn't find his cyanide capsule."

"What are you talking about?"

"Well," said Bérard, pronouncing each word carefully, "I won't be teaching you anything you don't already know. All the top leaders have a cyanide capsule. It's a well-known fact."

What Bérard wanted to say, since he represented the judiciary, was extremely clear to me and I answered him in the same vein.

"So, Judge, suppose we do a body search and don't find a cyanide capsule? Do you know where these can be obtained, because they certainly forgot to put one in my knapsack!"

The judge was stone faced when he answered me.

"Well, you figure that one out, old man. After all, you're the professional."

I paid a visit to Doctor P., a surgeon Mayer and I were friendly with. I knew I could count on his discretion. I had to explain that we were looking for cyanide to help a top FLN official commit suicide. He wrote a name and address on a visiting card.

"Tell him I sent you, he'll give you what you need."

With that strange prescription I went to the address of a pharmacy in Algiers. The pharmacist was a *pied-noir* and he couldn't help smiling when I explained what it was for.

"Are you in a big hurry?" he asked.

"No, no, not at all. Absolutely no hurry," I answered, looking absentminded.

"Then come back early tomorrow morning."

The next day he handed me a two-quart bottle of poison.

"But I can't use a bottle. A capsule is what I need! I'm not going to have him drink this!"

"That's your problem. This is all I can give you. All you have to do is hold him down and you'll see this stuff is absolutely lethal."

I kept that bottle for a long time at the Prefecture in our office, next door to Prefect Baret. Those who came in knew it was poison and the bottle became a standard joke.

"So, Aussaresses, always ready to buy someone a drink!"

Garcet was always having fun putting the bottle next to one of the bottles of scotch whiskey that had been brought back from Egypt. To his great amusement a visitor who had tried to pour himself a drink chose the wrong bottle and Garcet only prevented him from taking a deadly shot of poison at the very last second.

One morning I paid a visit to Bigeard's headquarters at El-Biar to meet Ben M'Hidi. Bigeard was with his deputy, Lenoir. They had the FLN leader brought in. A soldier served coffee with milk for everyone. Bigeard wanted to convince me that he had the situation under control and was successful in gaining the prisoner's trust. Everyone was trying to be very relaxed, but Bigeard was nervous. He knew he had to convince me that Ben M'Hidi was ready to collaborate with us. That was meaningless because our orders were to liquidate all the FLN leaders and that was my reason for being there. I felt Bigeard was losing his marbles.

"So, Ben M'Hidi what do you think about my regiment?" asked Bigeard.

"I think it's worth 300,000 men," answered Ben M'Hidi with a smile.

"And what do you think about your being arrested?"

Ben M'Hidi didn't know what to say. Bigeard decided to show his hand a bit more and went on:

"Don't you feel you've been betrayed?"

"And who could have betrayed me?" asked Ben M'Hidi.

"Well your colleagues at the CCE, for example. After all, they're Kabyles and you're an Arab."

Ben M'Hidi understood that Bigeard was trying to save his life and he had a sad smile.

"I wasn't betrayed, Colonel."

Bigeard then lost his cool somewhat.

"So how do you suppose we were able to catch you?"

"You were lucky, that's all."

In fact we had placed a tail on the son of millionaire Ben Tchicou, who owned a large tobacco company in Algiers and also managed the FLN's finances. Once he was arrested, Ben Tchicou, Jr. told us everything he knew, including Ben M'Hidi's address.

Bigeard was again attempting to help the prisoner.

"Why don't you work with us? Don't you think it would benefit your country if you joined up with France?"

"No, I don't think so."

"Well you can think what you want. I believe in a bigger France," concluded Bigeard, shrugging his shoulders.

Ben M'Hidi didn't want to cooperate and Bigeard knew full well what the consequences of such a refusal would be. Parat and Gévaudan, the police detectives of the criminal division, wanted Ben M'Hidi in the worst way, but Bigeard refused to hand him over because he knew they would have automatically tortured him. Parat was saying that Ben M'Hidi could be indicted for the murder of his opponents inside the FLN in western Algeria. Would he have talked under torture? We knew that Ben M'Hidi was responsible for most of the attacks and that he deserved the gallows ten times over, yet it wasn't absolutely certain that he would be found guilty in court.

On March 3, 1957 Massu and I discussed the problem in the presence of Trinquier. We agreed that a trial of Ben M'Hidi was not a good idea. There would have been international repercussions and we needed more time because we were hoping to bag the entire CCE. Ben M'Hidi hadn't betrayed his comrades but we found some very important clues in the documents found in his home.

"So what do you think?" asked Massu.

"I don't know why Ben M'Hidi should get preferential treatment compared to the other rebels. When it comes down to terrorism the leaders don't impress me any more favorably than their underlings. We've already executed many poor devils who were carrying out this guy's orders and here we are hesitating for three weeks just to find out what we're going to do about him!"

"I agree with you completely, but Ben M'Hidi is not just some cipher who will be quickly forgotten. We can't just make him simply disappear into thin air."

"There's no way we can hand him over to the police either. They claim they'll give him the third degree to make him talk but I'm convinced he won't say a word. If there were to be a trial and he hasn't confessed, he could actually walk away free, along with the entire FLN cadre. So let me take care of him before he becomes a fugitive, which is bound to happen if we keep on hesitating."

"Very well, go ahead and take care of him," answered Massu with a sigh. "Do the best you can. I'll cover you."

I understood that Massu already had the government's approval to proceed.

I picked up Ben M'Hidi the following night at El-Biar. Bigeard made sure he was somewhere else because he had been told ahead of time that I was coming to take the prisoner away. I came with a few Jeeps and a Dodge pick-up. There were about a dozen men from my first squad, all of them armed to the teeth. Captain Allaire was in charge and had a little combat group lined up and presenting arms. I asked him to go get Ben M'Hidi and hand him over to me.

"Present arms!" ordered Allaire, when Ben M'Hidi, who had just been awakened, was escorted out of the building.

To my amazement the paratroopers of the 3rd RPC gave the defeated FLN leader his final honors. It was Bigeard in effect paying his respects to a man who had become his friend. This spectacular and somewhat useless demonstration didn't make my job any easier. Obviously at that instant Ben M'Hidi fully understood what was in store for him. I quickly shoved him into the Dodge. We traveled very fast since an ambush to free him was always a possibility. I gave very strict orders to the NCO guard sitting next to the FLN leader:

"If we're ambushed, you shoot him immediately, even if we come out of this unharmed. Make sure you knock him off without hesitating!"

We stopped at an isolated farm that was occupied by the commando unit belonging to my regiment and located about twenty kilometers south of Algiers, on the left off the main road. A *pied-noir* had placed the farm at our disposal. It was a modest building and the living quarters were on the ground floor. My second team was waiting for us there.

The commando unit of the 1st RCP included about twenty men, some of whom were draftees, but all of them were completely reliable. Captain Allard, nicknamed Tatave, who was very much devoted to me, was in charge. I had told him what was going on and he had been briefed. I told him to have his men set up a corner of the room where Ben M'Hidi would be placed. The farm was messy and they had to move a few bales of hay around and sweep the floor. While this was taking place the prisoner was kept isolated in another room, which had been prepared. One of my men was standing guard at the door.

Then I entered with one of the soldiers and together we grabbed Ben M'Hidi and hanged him by the neck to make it look like suicide. Once I was sure he was dead, I immediately had him taken down and brought the body to the hospital. Following my orders, the NCO who was driving left the engine running while the car was parked, in order to be able to drive off at top speed without volunteering any explanations as soon as the emergency room doctor appeared. It was about midnight.

I immediately phoned Massu.

"General, Ben M'Hidi has just committed suicide. His body is at the hospital. I will bring you my report tomorrow."

Massu grunted and hung up the phone. He knew full well that my report had been ready since early afternoon, just to make sure. Judge Bérard was the first one to read it. It described in detail the suicide that was to take place the next night. Bérard was impressed:

"Well, this is very good! You know, it *does* make sense!"

Actually the report didn't make sense for very long. Massu called me to his office a few days later.

"Aussaresses, I'm in the shit. District Attorney Reliquet has called me in."

"What? He dared summon you?"

"Yes, to discuss the suicide of Ben M'Hidi."

"But that's an outrageous thing to do! Because of your position you shouldn't have to answer the summons. I'll go, since I'm your representative to the legal authorities."

I therefore paid a visit to the judge's office.

"Mr. District Attorney, I am here to represent General Massu. Because of my position I can discuss the circumstances of Ben M'Hidi's death. I'm also the author of the report that you've seen."

The district attorney was absolutely enraged.

"Yes, of course! Let's discuss your report! What you state in it is purely circumstantial. And *only* circumstantial! There's no proof. Can you military types offer any proof at all?"

"I can offer our good faith."

I think that had I slapped Reliquet across the face it would have had less of an impact than that answer.

"Your good faith!" he answered, choking on the words. "Your good faith as soldiers. Soldiers who are suddenly being candid?"

I put my beret back on, saluted him, clicking my heels, and walked out of the room.

We never heard from the attorney general again after that. The death of Ben M'Hidi was a decisive blow to the FLN in Algiers. The attacks died down and the bulk of the rebels began retreating toward the Atlas Mountains near Blida.

We used the farmhouse again where Ben M'Hidi had been executed. I had the men dig a long ditch and some twenty bodies, including that of a woman, were buried there.

16

Ali Boumendjel, Esq.

The 2nd RPC, under the command of Fossey-François, was informed that three French citizens had been murdered. A young couple and their small child had been shot south of Algiers while they were traveling on a motorcycle. Other Arabs had exposed the murderers, who were actually some local Arab thugs. "D," the regiment's intelligence officer, questioned the prisoners.

Before we executed them the contract killers admitted that the murder had been ordered and financed by Ali Boumendjel, a very successful attorney in Algiers, who was trying through this spectacular act to create an image for himself as a terrorist leader, instead of the café society intellectual everyone thought him to be. Like many other FLN leaders, such as Yacef Saadi, Boumendjel was annoyed by the popularity acquired by the small time crook named Ali-la-Pointe, who was portrayed as a kind of Algerian Robin Hood and always managed to elude our patrols because he was disguised as a woman.

Boumendjel was in our files; we knew he was an active FLN sympathizer. However, because of his many personal contacts among French government officials who were playing both sides, he had remained untouchable up to that time. His arrest, coming just a few days before that of Ben M'Hidi's, caused a big sensation. Attorney-at-law Ali Boumendjel had a brother who was also a lawyer and who proved to be amazingly efficient at getting the attention and enlisting support among liberal circles in Paris.

After an attempted suicide that landed him the hospital, Boumendjel immediately volunteered everything he knew—there was no need to use any violent methods to get him to talk—including his part in the murder for which he provided his personal automatic pistol to the killers. He also pointed out that he played an active and important role within the FLN, since he was in charge of the organization inside Algiers and also because he was responsible for FLN contacts with those foreign countries that were offering their support. He was acting as a foreign minister of sorts for the rebels.

Since Boumendjel was a well-known personality, no decision regarding his fate had been reached, even one week after his confession. He was still in the custody of the 2nd RPC. Because of his notoriety the most cautious scenario would have been to hand the attorney over to the judicial system, which meant, in effect, granting him impunity. The only charge against him was the minimum evidence that he had provided the weapon. He was an accomplice to a murder but there was absolutely no doubt that he would retract his confession the minute he faced the judge and would therefore be freed on bail once his brother started making a few phone calls.

A decision had to be made. On March 23, 1957 there was a long discussion between myself, Fossey-François, Trinquier, and Massu as to what was to be done with Ali Boumendjel. In my opinion, and despite all his important connections, which didn't impress me one bit, the lawyer was an out and out criminal who had ordered a disgusting murder for which the material killers had already been executed. The facts spoke clearly enough and the case was closed as far as I was concerned.

Since the discussion was not going anywhere I lost patience and got up, ready to walk out. Massu glared at me and then said:

"Aussaresses, he must not escape! I forbid it! Understood?"

Hearing those words I went straight to El-Biar, to the Boulevard Clemenceau where Boumendjel was being held. There were several buildings, some of them connected by footbridges at the sixth floor level where there were terraces. I walked into Lieutenant "D's" office. He was surprised to see me there.

"What can I do for you, Major?"

"Well 'D,' I'm here after a long meeting with General Massu. At the end of that long discussion I feel we can't keep Boumendjel in the building where he's being held right now."

"And why is that?"

"For many reasons. For instance, he might try to escape. Imagine how well that would go down! Massu would become rabid if that were to happen."

"So where should we put him?"

"I've thought the thing through. It would be best to transfer him to the building next door. But be very careful! To make the transfer you can't use the ground floor. That would attract too much attention."

"D" looked puzzled and couldn't quite fathom what I was hinting at, even though he sensed something.

"Major, please explain clearly what I'm supposed to do."

"It's very simple: you go get the prisoner and in order to transfer him to the building next door you use the 6th floor footbridge. I'll wait downstairs for you to be done. Do you understand me better now?"

"D" nodded to indicate he had understood, and walked away. I waited for a few minutes. "D" came back out of breath telling me that Boumendjel had fallen to his death. Before throwing him over the side of the footbridge "D" had knocked him out with a blow to the back of the head with a club. I rushed back in my jeep to see Massu and the others who were still debating the issue.

"General, you told me to make sure Boumendjel didn't escape. Well, he won't be able to because he just committed suicide."

As usual Massu just grunted his assent and I left the premises.

Boumendjel's death was to have huge repercussions and led to a lot of speculation in the press. The government, as is customary in such instances, demanded very vocally, and in so doing reached the heights of hypocrisy, a multitude of investigations and reports while the matter was being debated in parliament. I was fully aware of the campaigns by the Paris intelligentsia accusing the French army of using torture. I interpreted that kind of reaction clearly as a way of helping the FLN.

Yet Boumendjel's "suicide" was an occurrence that failed to deceive those who were better informed, and was actually a form of warning aimed at the FLN and its sympathizers. At first we had been knocking off the second fiddles. Now the man we had gone after was very well known. Many people understood that Boumendjel was tied to important people back in France and some of them had to be playing an active and important role in favor of the Algerian rebellion.

The jump from an Algerian to a well-known Frenchman was easy to make and I was determined to do so. Trinquier agreed with me on this.

The various autopsies and counter-autopsies that were ordered indicated that Boumendjel had "fallen and had been crushed to death by the impact" and that his body showed no traces of violence. I was never questioned and "D" kept repeating the official version of the attorney's inexplicable suicide. It was at the time of Boumendjel's death and because of the hysterical reactions it provoked in the circles favorable to the FLN in France that I really began thinking about the "suitcase carriers"—that was the nickname given to French nationals who volunteered to carry anywhere, including to Algeria, the money the FLN was gathering in France. There was no reason to treat them any better than the way we were treating the Muslim rebels. We had practically won the battle of Algiers. To terminate the FLN once and for all we also had to operate inside France itself.

17

A Battle We Won

In the spring of 1957 the daily newspaper *Le Monde* published an article by Eugène Mannoni on the front page: "The battle of Algiers ends in victory." This was not quite true by any means. The FLN had been defeated inside Algiers. We knew it because quite simply nothing was happening there anymore. The spectacular attacks had stopped and the arrests were dwindling. On some nights we came back without any prisoners. Algiers had become much too dangerous for the rebels, who were now falling back into the Atlas Mountains. I had even intercepted a letter written in French by a *fellagha* leader:

"My dear brother, I must get out of the Casbah, because for now, Massu has won. He's got it coming to him, that bastard!"

I proudly showed the article and the letter to Massu, who then decided to introduce Trinquier and me to Robert Lacoste. Yet not all the FLN leaders had left Algiers. Most of them were city dwellers who were living on the margins of society and were not about to pick up and take to the mountains. They often survived either by doing odd jobs or engaging in petty thievery, which made it impossible for them to leave town. The only way they would go was if they were forced to flee. We therefore had to hunt them down while they were still close at hand.

All we had to do was follow some paths leading to specific professions that were particularly sensitive, like the bricklayers for instance. Bigeard had created a list using information and professional registers provided by the Prefecture. Bricklayers were very much in demand to build weapons caches and hide explosive charges that were often walled off with masonry. We began checking and when we would run into a mason who had been out of work for a long time, according to the records, but whose hands indicated that he had just been working, he would then become one more suspect on our list.

Just as it appeared that the battle of Algiers was ending in victory for us, Colonel Godard suddenly reappeared. We had never seen him at the Prefecture during the toughest days but once he found out that Massu had appointed me to prepare the names of those who were to be candidates for citations for the military valor cross, Godard paid me a visit. The excuse was that he wanted to nominate a police inspector, whom I had never heard of before, for one of the citations.

"It would be very helpful to me," said Godard.

"If the citation is as useful to you as you claim, why don't you write it yourself instead of coming here asking me for favors?"

My answer was not the kind meant to improve our relationship.

There was one file that still bothered me a great deal, the one relating to the PCA, which we had left more or less untouched since the Bazooka case. I was convinced that the Communists were actively involved in manufacturing bombs that would certainly explode someday. Besides, the newspaper *La Voix du soldat* was still pursuing its insidious propaganda effort.

Massu, in agreement with the regimental commanders, had decided to reduce the military presence that had been set up within Algiers. From now on there would only be one regiment on location at any one time and each unit would take turns patrolling the city. The Algiers-Sahel sector under the command of Marey suddenly became very important. During the month of April, Suzanne Massu traveled to Paris where she had entrée into influential circles of society that hinted to her that her husband would be advised to relent somewhat in his persecution of the FLN. Upon her return to Algiers Suzanne described to her husband her conversations and the atmosphere she found in the French capital. Massu was becoming nervous and called Trinquier and me to a meeting to share his doubts and other worries. We had a long conversation about the matter.

"You realize that up there everyone is holding back," said Massu.

"Holding back about what?" I asked.

"Well, you have to understand: you're not in Paris, you're here in Algiers. People in Paris don't give a hoot about what's happening down here. And since you're in Algiers with a mission to enforce law and order, you shouldn't have to worry about what they're thinking."

Mrs. Massu had a lot of influence over the General, especially when she was trying to protect FLN women who were very few but who played an extremely important role. She thought that showing leniency toward some bomb-throwing women would possibly draw the sympathy of Algerian women to France. That was how she managed to prevent Djemila Bouhired, a law student who had been arrested on April 9, 1957 and who was guilty of participating in several attacks, from being put through the regular repressive cycle, meaning that Mrs. Massu feared that Djemila Bouhired would be sent to the villa des Tourelles. Because many people knew, and Suzanne Massu better than anyone else, that no terrorist who wound up there could expect any kind of leniency from me, regardless of sex, religion, or ethnic origin. The young woman was handed over to Captain Jean Graziani, Le Mire's deputy at the 2nd Bureau, whom Suzanne Massu considered a nice young man. It should be said that Djemila Bouhired revealed the location of a large bomb cache without having been tortured in any way.

Djemila Bouhired was extremely lucky because I would have not hesitated for one second to execute her. She was condemned to death on July 15, 1957, but was never executed. She was eventually set free and married her lawyer, Jacques Vergès, with whom she had several children. Following their divorce she went into business in Algiers.

Captain Graziani was far from being the tenderhearted type but he played the game according to the rules and was very courteous toward his prisoner. He even got her clothes and took her to the mess hall for dinner under the incredulous gaze of other officers. Thanks to Suzanne Massu the FLN women were almost systematically turned over to the justice system. By the end of the battle of Algiers, when I had already returned to my unit, I was told that a woman doctor had been arrested in the countryside on the same day as one of our officers had been savagely murdered. Massu had taken the initiative of evacuating the female prisoner by helicopter. As far as I was concerned it was no time to weaken. What we should have done was to finish the job and do away with the support the FLN was relying on inside France. Then I would have taken care of the Algerian Communists.

I felt like being all the more energetic, now that I could see that my mission was going to end soon. I had it in my mind to get everything done before the beginning of the summer. I spoke to Massu about it. He had no problem with my leaving, on condition that I find someone to replace me. That was no simple task because everyone knew that my mission was extremely difficult and there were no rivals envious enough to want my job. Had they polled the regiments for a replacement I'm sure no one would have stepped forward. So when I discreetly approached my comrades to measure their level of interest, all of them refused to even consider the possibility.

It was now May 1957. I was spending a lot of my time preparing in the greatest detail for our operations inside France itself. Trinquier and I were discussing these operations as we were planning them. I had prepared a very detailed operation to kill Ben Bella and his comrades within the CCE, namely Aït Ahmed Hocine, Mohammed Khider, Mohamed Boudiaf, and Mustafa Lacheraf. Ben Bella was destined, without a doubt, to play a major role should the FLN reach its objective and his elimination would have brought about terrible internal strife among the leadership. My conclusions were identical to those being reached within the executive branch of government by Max Lejeune, Maurice Bourgès-Maunoury, and Robert Lacoste.

After their arrest in October 1956, Ben Bella and his companions were taken to France. For security reasons Mitterrand had decided not to put them in prison, where they should have been kept, and instead had them transferred in absolute secrecy to a secure location in the provinces under heavy guard. I had found out from good sources that the FLN leader and his friends were living in excellent but not luxurious conditions. I was even able to put together a floor plan of the house where they were being held. All I needed was to have Massu agree to transfer five or six of my men to guard Ben Bella for one week. I was confident I could get his approval. He didn't need to know about the details of the actual operation. I had decided that the best thing would be a gas explosion, looking like an accident. The blast would blow away the buildings and we would disappear from the scene. Naturally I would have taken part in the operation myself with the help of the teams I had assigned. I put together this plan because I felt the battle of Algiers was now over and I could take some time away from the city for a few days.

I also wanted to deal a decisive blow to the FLN by attacking its financial lifelines, meaning the so-called "suitcase carriers." I was speaking confidentially to officials in

Paris and my teams in Algiers were ready to take covert action under my command. Money, as everyone knows, is the lifeline of war. It was one thing to sink the ships supplying the FLN with weapons or to blow up the arms merchants as the Action Service had been doing for three years. But to prevent the FLN from obtaining funds or shaking people down for the money it required to buy its weapons, there was another, more efficient, approach. Most of the funds came from France and in particular from Algerian workers and small businessmen who were quite simply subjected to widespread "protection" racketeering. Those who refused to pay up would have their throats slit or would be mowed down by submachine gun fire with the approval of some Frenchmen who favored the cause of the FLN.

The money was channeled through networks of volunteers who carried suitcases filled with banknotes. Obviously some suitcases disappeared once in a while. This was well known to the authorities but no one in Paris was handling the matter except for a small number of special Algerian policemen who specialized in taking brutal action against the FLN. The best known of the "suitcase" conveyors was the Jeanson network but there were others who were just as efficient. Perhaps there was no real political pressure to dismantle the networks since the FLN was clever enough to focus exclusively on Algerian Muslims. The money was used to buy weapons in Belgium, Switzerland, and Czechoslovakia that were then used against the French army, the *pieds-noirs*, and those Muslims who rejected the FLN.

Another portion of that money came from inside Algiers itself. Bigeard had uncovered some very large amounts when he had questioned Ben Tchicou. Massu had transferred the funds to charitable organizations working to help Algerian

Muslims inside France. It was fairly easy to take action against the suitcase conveyors. They were thoroughly convinced that they were doing the right thing, as they would still be years later when many were decorated for the services they rendered to Algeria; they benefited from the support of intellectuals and influential journalists and took very few precautions. Public opinion in France was rather indifferent to the war in Algeria, with the exception of the Algerian Muslims who were being shaken down inside the workplace and the parents of draftees who had been sent over as cannon fodder.

I had gathered some very detailed information about the suitcase carriers and those who supported them. These were sympathizers, such as Hervé Bourges, the journalist Olivier Todd, or the attorney Gisèle Halimi, for example, who had traveled to Algiers to meet with Suzanne Massu who had also practiced law. We found this out only at the last minute. I thought it was an unacceptable provocation and drove off with Garcet to intercept Halimi but we just missed her. I had established a list of about twelve names of people who should have been neutralized and with Trinquier I was putting together a detailed plan. These operations were to take place in Paris with a very small team and the targeted individuals were to be shot, execution style.

The string of deadly attacks in Algiers that took place on Monday, June 3, 1957, prevented the executions from taking place in Paris. Some people posing as employees of the EGA (*Électricité-Gaz d'Algérie*), sent by the team headed by Ali-la-Pointe, placed time bombs inside the street lights near three trolley car stations, setting the timers to blast during rush hour. This resulted in eight people being killed, including three children, and about 100 wounded; the victims of these attacks were evenly spread between Algerian Muslims and Europeans. During the evening of the following Sunday, June 9, the day of the feast of Pentecost, a 4½-pound bomb exploded under the orchestra platform at a dance club called Casino de la Corniche, located just 10 kilometers east of Algiers near Pointe-Pescade; the club catered exclusively to European youths. The extremely violent blast killed 9 persons and wounded 85 others. The musicians were blown to bits and the leader of the band basically disappeared, while the female singer lost both legs. It was the most spectacular of all the attacks and the one that affected me the most.

Massu was furious, even more so because the very next day the funeral of the victims became the scene of an unprecedented outbreak of wanton violence. We had to cordon off and protect the Casbah to prevent a bloodbath and perhaps even the fire that had been threatened. The day's toll was six people killed and fifty wounded, most of them Algerian Muslims. These attacks, coming after a long period without much violence, led us to increase our repressive action, starting with the Algerian Communist Party. We knew from our prior experience that the party included specialists in violent action and in particular chemists who were manufacturing bombs and those who provided weapons, such as Officer Cadet Maillot.

Out of the Night, a book by Jan Valtin, who was originally from Eastern Europe and had been closely associated with the Communists, had impressed me very much. It confirmed my deep-seated belief that structures were almost as important within the party as the ideology they intended to serve. What I knew about the Communist Party organization in general and the PCA in particular, proved to me that the various sections were separated by vertical and impenetrable firewalls. It was therefore possible for someone responsible at a very high level to meet another person in the same capacity but in another section; this would practically never happen at the grass roots.

Our intelligence was based on the extended use of files and information gathered from the start of the battle of Algiers and the census of the local population in particular. Non-paratrooper units could undertake similar operations. On June 10, 1957 a CRS sergeant, who was working with files set up by Roger Trinquier, intercepted a large sedan driven by Doctor Georges Hadjadj during a routine search. We had the doctor in our files as someone who could potentially be at a high level in the PCA's hierarchy. The sergeant escorted the Doctor to the nearest intelligence officer and Dr. Hadjadj readily admitted that he was an important leader of the party but denied having anything to do with the terrorist attacks. He claimed to be responsible only for handling the party's propaganda efforts, but he also confirmed that an Action Service did exist and that its leader was André Moine, just as I had suspected since early January. Dr. Hadjadj had met him during some party meetings but claimed not to know Moine's address or to be able to give more details about the Action Service.

Georges Hadjadj did say that within his area of responsibility he was in charge of the newspaper *La Voix du soldat*, and provided every conceivable detail about that activity. That information didn't further our investigation into the people responsible for the bomb attacks, but did allow me to reach one of the objectives set by Massu. The name of Maurice Audin appeared among the doctor's papers and that name was also carried on our lists. Hadjadj volunteered information that Audin, a young mathematics professor and a leader inside the PCA, provided his home as a safe house for party agents, which meant that he could easily have as his guest an active member of the Action Service. Hadjadj gave us Audin's address, which was in Charbonnier's sector, and this allowed the men of the 1st RCP to go and pick him up. I was informed of the arrest and immediately went over to Audin's apartment, where I hoped to discover André Moine's address.

Later on Henri Alleg, the former editor of the Communist daily *Alger républicain*, fell into a trap as he entered Audin's apartment. As far as I was concerned neither Audin nor Alleg was that important, even though their names were in the file. I returned to Audin's apartment after Alleg had been captured and asked Charbonnier to question both men to find out if they belonged to the Action Service of the PCA and use the papers and address books they had at home to look for André Moine's name.

As some may remember, Audin vanished on June 21 and his disappearance caused a lot of indignation and became the object of a very detailed investigation. As for Alleg, he wrote a book, *La Question*, describing his interrogation. I saw him when he was placed under arrest but he failed to mention that fact in his book, which otherwise spares the reader no details. The Alleg and Audin cases became sensational in France because of the interpretation provided by the Communist Party and the newspapers supporting the FLN.

By then I was reaching the end of six months on a temporary mission that would have automatically become permanent after that time—something I didn't want. I felt I had fully accomplished what I had been asked to do: the strike had been broken, the files had been created, and *La Voix du soldat* was silent. Even more importantly, Larbi Ben M'Hidi and Ali Boumendjel had been executed and I had set up the procedure so that the others would meet the same fate. With Massu's support Godard had been given command of the Algiers-Sahel sector so that from now on he could keep an eye on whatever we were doing. That new development encouraged me to leave my command as quickly as possible and find someone to take over my position.

I found the man in Captain Jacques de La Bourdonnaye-Monluc, who was in command of the marching unit of the 11th Shock battalion stationed on the outskirts of Algiers. He had been with me in Indochina and part of the 1st RCP. He was in a tough position because his commanding officer in Algeria, Decorse, had placed his name at the top of the "osmosis" list, which precluded his remaining in a paratrooper unit. So La Bourdonnaye-Monluc was supposed to change units, leave the paratroopers and the city of Algiers, and transfer to the 44th Infantry regiment operating on the border with Tunisia. The advantage of being posted with General Massu was that he would remain in Algiers, something he preferred for personal reasons, and retain his status as a paratrooper, which he wanted even more.

At first La Bourdonnaye-Monluc didn't appear too enthusiastic. The 1st RCP arrived to take over security within Algiers and I invited him to the mess hall to meet with Prosper and Monette Mayer. Together we were able to convince him to accept. I could not get along with Godard and therefore it was impossible for me to continue on that mission. Godard was also nervous about the fact that we were pursuing the Communists and setting up plans to act against

French citizens. He also managed to get rid of Trinquier, who was given orders to transfer to a new unit within 48 hours. So I sent La Bourdonnaye-Monluc to report to Godard and, since the two men got along quite well, within a week the transfer became effective and he took over my team. I was then able to tell Massu that I had found an officer to replace me and that as far as I was concerned the battle of Algiers was over.

18

The *Deserter*

The 1st RCP was garrisoned at Maison-Carrée and I returned to the unit as chief of staff, the posting I had at the beginning of the year. I was relieved. The loneliness I had experienced during those six months was no longer bearable. Now I could go to war out in the open and chase the FLN in the Atlas Mountains of Blida. Babaye asked to follow me and I couldn't refuse his request. During the first firefight I gave him a rifle and told him to stay quietly behind me. Very soon I heard a shot coming from the back and a bullet whizzed close to my ears. I turned around and saw that Babaye was laughing. He had just fired over my shoulder and killed an enemy I hadn't seen.

At that time the last FLN leaders in Algiers and the heads of the PCA were dropping one after the other. Faulques, the intelligence officer, had the excellent idea of posting names on the doors of the empty cells in the basement of Villa Sésini. He posted the name of André Moine and this led the other prisoners to believe that Moine had been captured. In fact, this finally led to his being apprehended in July 1957.

The plan to get close enough to Yacef Saadi, that I had patiently elaborated with the help of my deep penetration agent inside the FLN, was finally enacted by Faulques, La Bourdonnaye, and Godard in September. The 1st REP under Jeanpierre's command was able to surround the villa where Yacef was hiding. He defended himself by throwing a hand grenade. Jeanpierre was wounded but the Foreign Legionnaires captured Yacef Saadi, who confessed spontaneously, and that saved his life. He revealed the address of Ali-la-Pointe, who was hiding in a fortified house inside the Casbah. Ali-la-Pointe's popularity bothered Yacef Saadi as much as it had annoyed Ali Boumendjel in the past.

On October 8, 1957 the bunker of Ali-la-Pointe was located and carefully surrounded. We sent in the sappers of the engineers battalion to blast open a passageway, but the lieutenant placed an explosive charge that was too strong and wound up reducing the bunker to rubble, as well as six houses close by. We identified the body of Ali-la-Pointe because of a tattoo he had on his foot. The young woman and a little boy, who served as a messenger and who lived with Ali, were also killed in the explosion. That event marked the end of the battle of Algiers.

Paul Teitgen had addressed a report to Robert Lacoste on March 29, 1957, handing in his resignation because he suspected that the army was using torture. His resignation had been refused and he remained at his post until October 8, 1957. For the second time, in view of the situation, Paul Teitgen decided resign, and that was now accepted. He calculated that the total number of persons arrested was over 24,000. By adding the number of persons arrested during the battle of Algiers and subtracting those who were still being held in the camps or who had since been released, Paul Teitgen came to the conclusion that 3,024 persons were missing.

In the fall of 1957 I was transferred to Baden-Baden as an airborne support instructor. However, I returned to Algeria several times after that to organize training exercises. The ALN had concentrated some large forces in camps in Tunisia very close to the Algerian border. It was very clever, since France had recognized the autonomy of Tunisia in the spring of 1956. The camps were used to organize attacks against our border positions. At the beginning of 1958 two French planes were shot down by anti-aircraft fire and some draftees had been massacred. A bombing raid was organized in retaliation on the other side of the border on February 8, 1958. During the raid the Tunisian village of Sakiet Sidi Youssef was bombed and the incident had such disastrous international repercussions that France was compelled to accept an American good will mission. The French army could thereafter no longer cross the border and the ALN was able to resume its attacks undeterred. ALN forces had also withdrawn far enough from the frontier line to feel completely safe. Thanks to a pilot who flew me discreetly in a T6 reconnaissance plane up to the border and before penetrating Tunisian air space, we were able to elude the anti-aircraft shelling and fire rockets and machine guns against

ALN positions. Those raids were never officially acknowledged.

Babaye married the daughter of a local park policeman. In 1962, when the French army was about to leave, his former friends inside the FLN let him know that they bore no grudges and wished him to remain in Algeria, but a French army colonel forced him and his family to take the last ship leaving for France. Kemal Issolah was recognized and arrested by the FLN. I was able to free him and have him exfiltrated with the help of a U.S. military attaché in Algiers.

In the fall of 1966, after having served as instructor at Fort Benning, Georgia, and Fort Bragg, North Carolina, for U.S. Special Forces being trained for action in Vietnam and having worked as a staff officer, I was eager to return to my old unit, the 1st RCP, now back home in Pau. This time I took command, following in the footsteps of Cockborne and Prosper. In the evening they gave a party and I asked the military band to play *Le Déserteur*, the song written by Boris Vian that I was humming eleven years earlier when I arrived at Philippeville. Now I was a Lieutenant Colonel and my reputation as an eccentric was fully justified. Much to my surprise the request didn't shock anyone and even amused many younger officers who hadn't served in Algeria.

As I watched them dance I thought back to El-Halia, the villa des Tourelles, the attacks at the stadium, to Ben M'Hidi, the bobby-trapped street lights, Boumendjel, the casino of the Corniche, and all those endless nights. I had no regrets but I did make a wish that none of these young men would ever have to do some day for my country what I had to do over there, in Algeria.

Glossary

ADC   Aide-de-camp.

ALAT   *Aviation légère de l'armée de terre* – light army aircraft, mainly the T6 single engine reconnaissance planes also used in combat.

Algérie Française   Rallying cry for those in favor of continued French rule and opposed to independence for Algeria.

ALN   *Armée de Libération Nationale*; military formations of the FLN mostly stationed in Tunisia.

Arab   The ethnic majority of the Algerian population living mostly in cities and towns; French speakers generally refer to Algerians as "Arabs."

Aurès Mountains	Mountain chain crossing most of eastern Algeria in the area around Constantine.
babaye	Arabic slang for black Africans.
barbouze	Colloquial nickname given to secret agents thought to use a false beard.
BCRA	*Bureau central de renseignement et d'action*; intelligence unit of the Free French in London under the command of General de Gaulle, 1940-1945.
Berber	Largest non-Arab minority living in the mountains and mostly rural areas; speak many different dialects.
Blida	Small town located southwest of Algiers.
Bône	Main city on the eastern Algerian coast, now called Annaba.
Boufarik	Town located south of Algiers.
CCE	*Comité de Coordination et d'Exécution*; main terrorist arm of the FLN inside Algiers, led by Larbi Ben M'Hidi.
Charlemagne SS Division	A division of French volunteers in the Waffen SS operating on the Russian front with the approval of the Vichy government.

CRS   *Compagnies Républicaines de Sécurité*; French
                        riot police.

Deuxième Bureau   Also written 2ème Bureau; French mili-
                        tary intelligence, equivalent of the U.S.
                        G-2.

DGSE   *Direction générale de la sécurité extérieure*; cre-
                        ated in 1981; the successor agency of the
                        SDECE, in charge of all French foreign
                        espionage.

Dien Bien Phu   Valley in North Vietnam near the Lao-
                        tian border that came under siege, end-
                        ing in defeat for 16,000 French forces
                        from 1953 until its fall to the Viet Minh
                        troops of Vo Nguyen Giap on May 7,
                        1954, concluding the war for the inde-
                        pendence of Indochina from French rule.

DP   *Division Parachutiste* (airborne division).

DPU   *Détachment de Protection Urbaine* (units tak-
                        ing census of the population.

EGA   *Électricité-Gaz d'Algérie* (main public util-
                        ity).

Europeans   Generic term to identify all non-Arabs,
                        whether they are *pieds-noirs* or not.

FLN   *Front de Libération Nationale*; National lib-
                        eration front, the main Algerian nation-
                        alist political movement created in 1954.

Fourth Republic	Founded in 1946; lasted until 1959 when General de Gaulle inaugurated the Fifth Republic and a new constitution.
GCMA	*Groupment de Combat Mixte Aéroporté* (airborne fighter group).
gégène	Slang for electric shocks applied to the prisoners to force them to talk.
Gendarmerie	Local French police force.
Harkis	Algerian Muslims enrolled as auxiliary forces in the French army; were considered traitors by the FLN; many were murdered in 1962-63 when Algeria became independent.
Jedburgh	Code name given to special 3-man allied commando units (one man being a radio operator), organized by British intelligence to operate behind German lines in occupied Europe during World War II.
Kabyle	Non-Arab minority speaking the Kabyle language, a Berber dialect.
Kabylie	Mountain region located southeast of Algiers; populated by a non-Arab ethnic group speaking Kabyle.
Maghreb	Geographic term designating three countries in North Africa: Morocco, Algeria, and Tunisia.

Maquis   Literally "the bush"; name of partisan groups in France and elsewhere, originally coined during World War Two.

Milice   Paramilitary police force set up by the Vichy government to fight Resistance partisans of the *maquis*; known to be particularly brutal.

MNA   *Movement Nationaliste Algérien*; rival nationalist party of the FLN founded by Messali Hadj in December 1954.

MTLD   *Mouvement pour le Triomphe des Libertés Démocratiques*; nationalist party founded by Messali Hadj after 1945; became the MNA.

Muslim   French writers often refer to Arab Algerians as "Muslims" to distinguish them from Europeans.

NCO   Non-commissioned officer.

NKVD   Abbreviation of Soviet intelligence; eventually became the KGB in 1946.

11th Shock Battalion   11ème Choc; commando formation within the SDECE in charge of dirty tricks and perilous missions.

Oued Zem   Small village inside Morocco where all 49 French inhabitants were massacred on August 20, 1955, including 8 women and

15 children; patients in the local hospital and the doctor were also horribly murdered. The Foreign Legion retaliated, brutally killing an estimated 2,000 Moroccans.

pastis	Anisette drink, popular in most of French North Africa and southern France.
Paul-Cazelles	Small town south of Algiers, renamed Aïn Oussera.
PCA	*Parti Communiste Algérien*; Algerian Communist Party.
Philippeville	Mid-size town on the eastern Algerian coast, now named Skikda.
Pieds-noirs	Literally "black feet"; nickname originally given by Arabs to French settlers who first arrived wearing black leather shoes.
Préfecture	Main local administrative unit of the French state reporting to the Ministry of the Interior, who names the Préfet acting as the local representative of the central government.
Police Judiciaire	Also known as PJ; the criminal police division within the Préfecture, equivalent of the Homicide Squad in the U.S.
RCA	*Régiment de Cavalerie Africaine*—African Cavalry Regiment.

RCP	*Régiment de Chasseurs Parachutistes*; regular paratroopers.
Renseignements Généraux	Also referred to as RG; the intelligence service of the local police forces at the level of the Préfecture.
REP	*Régiment Étranger de Parachutistes*; Foreign Legion paratroopers.
Rif War	Long guerilla conflict in the mountains of Northern Morocco, lasting from 1921 to the 1930s, where the French army suffered 37,000 dead.
RPC	*Régiment de Parachutistes Coloniaux*; colonial paratroopers in Indochina; also known as the "berets rouges," the red berets.
Route Coloniale Numéro 4	Also known as RC4; a key road in French Indochina that was the scene of heavy fighting and losses by French forces.
SAS	*Sections Administratives Spécialisées*; French military units dedicated to providing services to the Algerian Muslim population.
SDECE	*Service de Documentation Extérieure et de Contre-Espionnage*; French foreign intelligence agency, equivalent to the British MI6 and the American CIA, created in 1945.

Service Action	Secret intervention unit of the SDECE; authorized to operate secretly outside France and undertake violent action against persons and property that could endanger the French Republic; included commando and other sabotage units like the 11ème Choc, which was created by General Aussaresses in 1946.
Services Spéciaux	Special Services; overall term describing all intelligence functions of the Ministry of Defense.
Sétif	Small town in the Kabylie Mountains, scene of the first large-scale violent revolt on May 8, 1945 by pro-independence Algerians, where about 100 French settlers and between 3,000 and 6,000 Algerian Muslims were killed.
Viet Minh	Nationalist movement in Indochina, led by Ho Chi Minh, operating in Vietnam fighting against the French army.
ZAA	*Zone Autonome d'Alger*, secretly set up as the FLN autonomous zone of the city of Algiers.

Biographical sketches

Ali-la-Pointe
Alias of Ali Amar, a young Casbah pimp and key terrorist working with Yacef Saadi; murdered Amédée Froger in December 1956; killed in an explosion set by paratroopers in the Casbah in October 1957.

Ferhat Abbas
Pharmacist from Sétif who spoke French almost exclusively; moderate nationalist political leader, elected to the French parliament in 1946; joined the FLN in 1956, became first president of the Algerian provisional government in exile in Tunis; expelled from the FLN in 1963 after Algerian independence.

Antoine Argoud
Colonel in command of the district south of Algiers known for his very tough approach to the FLN; General Massu's chief of staff in 1959; later joined the OAS.

Jo Attia	Parisian gangster, a member of the so-called "traction avant gang" led by Pierrot-le-Fou in the late 1940s; former Resistance fighter; survived Mauthausen concentration camp; employed by Jacques Morlanne as agent of the SDECE; failed to arrange the murder of Moroccan nationalist leader Allal El Fassi in 1956; imprisoned in Morocco, then released to France where he continued his mob activities.
Ahmed Ben Bella	One of the historical leaders of the FLN; joined the MTLD in 1945, arrested for a bank robbery in 1950, escaped from a French prison to Cairo in 1952; founding member of the FLN, created in October 1954; arrested with four other Algerian leaders in October 1956 when his plane was forced to land in Algiers; freed in 1962, became the first president of the Algerian Republic; later overthrown in a military coup in 1965.
Marcel Bigeard	Colonel in command of the 3rd RPC, rose through the ranks after World War II; hero of Dien Bien Phu; captured by the Viet Minh and released; conducted many successful operations in Algeria and during the battle of Algiers.
Jean Pâris de Bollardière	General; openly opposed to torture; was placed under house arrest in January 1957 by Massu.

Djamila Bouhired	One of the young women working for Yacef Saadi in the Casbah; placed several bombs and recruited other women; arrested in April 1957; sentenced to death and reprieved; married and divorced attorney Jacques Vergès, who also was the lawyer for the terrorist Carlos the Jackal.
Ali Boumendjel	Lawyer and FLN sympathizer; arrested in February 1957; organized the murder of a young French family to ingratiate himself with FLN leaders; executed on orders from General Aussaresses.
Maurice Bourgès-Maunoury	Minister of the Interior in the government of Edgar Faure; became Defense Minister in the government of Guy Mollet; Prime Minister from May to November 1957; prime mover of the hard line taken against the Algerian rebels.
Georges Catroux	General; former French high commissioner to Syria and Lebanon, where he favored independence; was 79 years old in 1956; appointed by Guy Mollet as Minister in Residence in Algeria; rejected by the *pieds-noirs* as favorable to independence; resigned in the face of popular protest in February 1956.
Edgar Faure	Legal scholar and key politician of the Fourth Republic; Prime Minister from February 1955 to January 1956; negotiated independence for Morocco and Tunisia and

pursued a hard line policy in Algeria; dissolved parliament in December 1955; paving the way for the socialist government of Guy Mollet.

Jacques Foccart — Resistance fighter; lieutenant colonel in de Gaulle's Free French army; influential advisor to de Gaulle from 1944 to 1969 for intelligence matters and his personal liaison to the SDECE; undersecretary for African affairs from 1958 until his retirement.

Charles de Gaulle — French army general; Saint-Cyr graduate; Undersecretary of War in the last government of the Third Republic in June 1940; leader of the Free French in London; President of the Provisional Government in 1944-1946; returned to power in 1958 with the support of the army and the *pieds-noirs*; later switched his policy to granting independence to Algeria in 1962; President of France until his resignation in 1969.

Yves Godard — Colonel; commander of the 11th Shock battalion after Aussaresses in 1948; saw action in Indochina; chief of staff to General Massu during the battle of Algiers as intelligence chief; later became a leader of the OAS.

Messali Hadj — Long-time Algerian nationalist leader; founder of various nationalist movements in the 1930s; in 1945 founded the MTLD, which changed its name to MNA in Deccmber 1954; often imprisoned by French authorities, he was consistently opposed to both the FLN and to French policies.

Nikolaus Lenau full name: Nikolaus Niembsch von Strehlenau (1802-1850); Austrian poet and a favorite of Paul Aussaresses.

Jacques Massu General; joined the Free French in the Second World War; fought in France and Germany; took part in the war in Indochina; commander of the 10th DP (10th Paratrooper Division); named Prefect of Algiers in 1956; main officer in charge of counterterrorist repression; took part in the overthrow of the Fourth Republic and supported the return of de Gaulle in 1958.

Pierre
Mendès-France French Prime minister from June 1954 to February 1955; negotiated the peace agreement in Indochina, and the preliminary independence steps with Morocco and Tunisia vowing to stand firm in Algeria; favored a liberal policy in Algeria; resigned from the Guy Mollet government in May 1956 because of disagreements on a tougher Algerian policy.

François
Mitterrand Moderate socialist; a cabinet minister in several governments of the Fourth Republic; Minister of the Interior in the Mendès-France government, responsible for the first

policies in Algeria when the rebellion began in 1954; later Minister of Justice in
the government of Edgar Faure in 1955;
became President of France in 1981.

Larbi Ben M'Hidi   One of the historical leaders of the FLN;
organized the network of terror inside the
city of Algiers; main mover behind the
failed general strike of January 1957; arrested by Colonel Marcel Bigeard's paratroopers; executed by hanging, personally
carried out by General Aussaresses; death
was always ruled a suicide until now.

Mohamed V   Also known as Sidi Mohamed Ben Youssef;
Sultan, then King, of Morocco until his
death in 1961; moderately favorable to the
nationalists, he was deposed by French administrators and southern Berber tribesmen
on August 20, 1953; sent into exile to Madagascar; returned to Morocco and obtained
independence from France in March 1956.

Guy Mollet   Leader of the French Socialist party; Prime
Minister from January 1956 to May 1957;
pursued a tough policy against the FLN in
Algeria; also led the Suez expedition against
Nasser in Egypt, along with Great Britain
and Israel.

Jacques Morlanne   Colonel; real name Henri Fille-Lambie;
head of the Action Service of the SDECE
and commanding officer of Paul Aussaresses;
held responsible for the failure of Jo Attia;
relieved of his command in 1958.

178

Gamal
Abdel Nasser

Colonel in the Egyptian army; one of the leaders of the officer's revolt against the monarchy in 1952; became president of Egypt; staunch supporter of Arab nationalist movements; nationalized the Suez Canal, bringing about the French-British-Israeli attack in November 1956.

Robert Lacoste

Socialist party official; appointed Minister in Residence for Algeria after the resignation of General Catroux in February 1956; pursued tough counter-terrorist policies from February 1956 to May 1958.

Max Lejeune

Undersecretary of War reporting to Minister Bourgès-Maunoury in the government of Guy Mollet; responsible for the counterterrorist policies; covered and authorized the use of torture and executions, main mover of the arrest of Ahmed Ben Bella and his companions in October 1956.

Yacef Saadi

Baker in the Casbah and key member of the CCE under Larbi Ben M'Hidi; headed a terror network of about 1,400 operatives, including young women like Djamila Bouhired; arrested in 1957 at the end of the battle of Algiers; accused by General Aussaresses of revealing the hiding place of Ali-la-Pointe to French intelligence.

Raoul Salan

General; former French army commander in Indochina; intelligence specialist; commander in chief of the 10th military region covering Algeria 1956-1959; in 1961 led a failed military coup against de Gaulle's government; leader of the OAS; condemned to death in absentia, then amnestied by General de Gaulle.

Roger Trinquier   Colonel; served in Asia from 1938 to 1954; specialist in psychological warfare; spent years fighting behind Viet Minh lines in Indochina; main intelligence officer with Paul Aussaresses on General Massu's secret staff; later became a mercenary in the Katanga.

INDEX

Acknowledgements

Sylvie Bréguet of Editions Perrin; Claude Ribbe; Peter Klein and Trisha Sorrells of *60 Minutes*; Matthew Teague; Richard Valcourt; Charles Miller; Catherine Dop; Roland Winter; Asya Kunik; Jay Wynshaw.